Nationalizing Influences
on
Secondary Education

Edited by

Roald F. Campbell
Director

Robert A. Bunnell
Staff Associate

Midwest Administration Center

THE UNIVERSITY OF CHICAGO

PUBLISHED AND COPYRIGHTED
FEBRUARY, 1963

MIDWEST ADMINISTRATION CENTER
THE UNIVERSITY OF CHICAGO
5835 SOUTH KIMBARK AVENUE
CHICAGO 37, ILLINOIS

LIBRARY OF CONGRESS CATALOG CARD NUMBER LC 63-11932

Printed by Interstate Printers and Publishers, Inc., Danville, Illinois, U.S.A.

PREFACE

The American people have had a tendency to take for granted any of their hard-won, free institutions that are not at the moment at the center of some political, social, or economic crisis. The maximum national effort required to meet the challenge of World War II reinforced a national approach to problems that has had some recurring historical appeal. With the increase of international tensions following the official cessation of hostilities, an emphasis on national solutions has continued. Education is one of our institutions that is no longer taken for granted but has come to be seen as contributing to, as well as being a part of the remedy for, the uncertainties that we face as a nation. Thus, the demand for national solutions to educational problems has lead to the creation of influential programs unknown to previous generations. The purpose of this monograph, then, is to bring together a number of studies that bear on the nationalizing influences that have become more and more pervasive in their effects on secondary education.

Staff members of the Midwest Administration Center have given considerable attention to this problem. During the 1961-1962 academic year, a graduate seminar sponsored by the Center focused on this problem. The general outline of this monograph, and the research behind Chapters 2 and 7 came out of the seminar which included in its membership the editors as well as the following: Arthur Kratzmann, Kenton Stephens, Robert W. Nesper, Robert Perz, Stanley T. Ptak, and Lester Przewlocki. Roy A. Larmee, Assistant Professor of Education, also participated in the seminar and contributed a summary of his dissertation research to this publication.

Other research on nationalizing influences was begun prior to the seminar by Lorraine M. LaVigne, Principal of the Bradwell School in Chicago, and Lloyd J. Mendelson, Principal of the Farren School in Chicago, and following the completion of their dissertations in the summer of 1962 they consented to prepare chapters for this monograph. A sincere debt of gratitude is owed to all of these people for their cooperation and interest in getting the chapters written, and their willingness to check additional sources for the most recent information. And we would like to thank publicly the many administrators and teachers of the public and private schools who were interested enough in our problem to give us information and reasoned judgments. We bear the responsibility for the accuracy of the reporting.

Since the topic discussed here is capable of raising emotional

PREFACE

reactions which may interfere with the perception of facts, one caveat seems in order. There is no "party line" endorsed by the Midwest Administration Center and promulgated here. Each of the chapters was independently authored, and no uniformity of conclusion or inference was made a condition of publication. Our goals are a wider awareness of the trends we believe are demonstrated here, and a willingness on the part of all who follow education as their profession to make an effort to understand these and many other nationalizing forces so they can better take the action that the times demand.

The University of Chicago   R.F.C.
January, 1963   R.A.B.

TABLE OF CONTENTS

		Page
1.	**The Problem**	
	by Kenton Stephens	1
	An Historical Note	5
	The Guiding Questions	10
2.	**Exploratory Studies**	
	by Roald F. Campbell	13
	Findings	15
	Conclusions	20
3.	**The National Science Foundation**	
	by Lloyd J. Mendelson	25
	Historical Background	26
	The National Science Foundation Act	28
	Influences on Secondary Education	32
	The Process of Educational Policy Making	36
	Conclusions and Implications	38
4.	**The National Merit Scholarship Program**	
	by Lorraine LaVigne	41
	Background and Problem	41
	Methodology	43
	Findings	45
	Conclusions	54
5.	**The National Defense Education Act of 1958**	
	by Arthur Kratzmann	57
	Antecedent Forces	57
	Provisions and Implementation of the Act	60
	Reactions to the Act	65
	Some Pertinent Questions	69
	Summary	71
6.	**The College Entrance Examination Board**	
	by Lester Przewlocki	73
	Background	73
	Entrance Testing	75
	College Scholarship Service	78
	Advanced Placement Programs	78
	Problems and Prospects	81

TABLE OF CONTENTS

                                                                           Page

7. **The Impact on Public High Schools**
      by Stanley Ptak and Robert Bunnell   85
   The National Science Foundation   87
   The National Defense Education Act   91
   The College Entrance Examination Board   97
   The National Merit Scholarship Program   100
   Summary and Conclusions   102

8. **National Movements and Independent Schools**
      by Roy A. Larmee   105
   The Programs   108
   The Schools and the Programs   110
   The Schools and Program Development   112
   Conclusions   114

9. **Impact and Implications**
      by Roald F. Campbell and Robert Bunnell   119
   Impact   120
   Conclusions   124
   Some Implications   126

LIST OF TABLES

1. Characteristics of Secondary Schools in Which Case Studies Were Done   14
2. Obligations of the National Science Foundation in Support of Education in the Sciences, 1952-1962   30
3. National Science Foundation Allocation of Funds for Science Education, Fiscal Year 1962   31
4. Growth of the National Merit Scholarship Program   50
5. Number of Schools Reporting Level of Success in the National Merit Scholarship Program by Socio-Economic Class Level of Community Inhabitants   53
6. NDEA Authorizations and Appropriations for Fiscal Years 1959 through 1962   62
7. Educational Testing Service Programs Conducted for the College Entrance Examination Board, 1947-1961   83
8. The National Science Foundation Programs: Participation and Effects Reported by Illinois Public High Schools (Percentages Reported by Socio-Economic Level)   88
9. The National Science Foundation Programs: Participation and Effects Reported by Illinois Public High Schools (Percentages Reported by Location)   89

LIST OF TABLES

	Page
10. The National Science Foundation Programs: Participation and Effects Reported by Illinois Public High Schools (Percentages Reported by Size within Specific Locations)	90
11. The National Science Foundation Programs: Judgments of Effects on School (Percentages Reported by Socio-Economic Level, Size, and Location)	90
12. The National Defense Education Act: Participation and Effects Reported by Illinois Public High Schools (Percentages Reported by Socio-Economic Level)	92
13. The National Defense Education Act: Participation and Effects Reported by Illinois Public High Schools (Percentages Reported by Location)	93
14. The National Defense Education Act: Participation and Effects Reported by Illinois Public High Schools (Percentages Reported by Size within Specific Locations)	95
15. The National Defense Education Act: Judgments of Effects on School (Percentages Reported by Socio-Economic Level, Size, and Location)	96
16. The College Entrance Examination Board: Participation and Preparation Reported by Illinois Public High Schools (Percentages Reported by Socio-Economic Level)	98
17. The College Entrance Examination Board: Participation and Preparation Reported by Illinois Public High Schools (Percentages Reported by Location)	98
18. The College Entrance Examination Board: Participation and Preparation Reported by Illinois Public High Schools (Percentages Reported by Size within Specific Locations)	99
19. The College Entrance Examination Board: Judgments of Effects on School (Percentages Reported by Socio-Economic Level, Size, and Location)	99
20. The National Merit Scholarship Program: Participation and Preparation Reported by Illinois Public High Schools (Percentages by Socio-Economic Level, Size, and Location)	100
21. The National Merit Scholarship Program: Judgments of Effects on School (Percentages Reported by Socio-Economic Level, Size, and Location)	101
22. The Involvement of the Eleven Independent Schools in the Origin of the Advanced Placement Program and in the 1961 Examination and Reading Committees	113
23. Leadership Positions in the Five Curriculum Programs Which Were Filled from the Eleven Schools	115

OTHER STUDIES IN EDUCATIONAL ADMINISTRATION

School Finance and Local Planning, by John G. Fowlkes and George E. Watson. 1957. 85 pp. $2.00.

School Board Studies, by Maurice E. Stapley. 1957. 56 pp. $2.00.

School District Reorganization, by L. L. Chisholm. (out of print)

Administrative Relationships, by Egon G. Guba and Charles E. Bidwell. 1957. 118 pp. $2.00.

Consultative Services to Local School Systems, by William W. Savage. 1959. 74 pp. $2.00.

Administrative Theory in Education, edited by Andrew W. Halpin. Sponsored by the University Council for Educational Administration and the Midwest Administration Center. 1958. 188 pp. $3.00.

The Leadership Behavior of School Superintendents, by Andrew W. Halpin. Originally published by College of Education, The Ohio State University, 1956. Second Printing by the Midwest Administration Center, The University of Chicago. 1959. 109 pp. $2.00.

The Task of Public Education, by Lawrence W. Downey. 1960. 88 pp. $2.00.

Administrative Theory as a Guide to Action, edited by Roald F. Campbell and James M. Lipham. 1960. 205 pp., hardbound. $3.50.

Executive Succession and Organizational Change, by Richard O. Carlson. 1961. 84 pp. $2.50.

Copies of these publications may be obtained from:

Midwest Administration Center
The University of Chicago
5835 Kimbark Avenue
Chicago 37, Illinois

The Problem

Kenton Stephens

Chapter 1

Many Americans would hold that the local management of public schools is best. The intrusion of other levels of government on local operation is often looked upon with disfavor. Action by the Federal government is the most suspect, but even the states, which legally have plenary power with respect to education, are not always welcome in their endeavors to control education. Preoccupation with governmental control of education may actually blind citizens to the variety of nongovernmental agencies affecting education, most of which are organized nationally.

The purpose of this monograph is to examine the extent to which public schools are influenced in their policies and programs by national agencies, both governmental and nongovernmental. With so little known about the nature and extent of the influences impinging upon American education, it was felt that it would be useful to compile under one cover reports of a series of relevant investigations.

Even though very little systematic study has taken place concerning national forces affecting schools, there is a plethora of comment concerning the kinds of forces which should (or should not) control the schools. In his message on education to the Congress of the United States, February 6, 1962, President Kennedy said,

> The control and operation of education in America must remain the responsibility of state and local governments and private institutions. This tradition assures our educational system of the freedom, the diversity and the vitality in support of public elementary and secondary education.[1]

This remark by the President appeared in a message advocating greatly expanded federal activities in support of public elementary

---

[1] U. S., *Congressional Record*, 87th Cong., 2d Sess., 1962, CVIII, 1544.

2   Nationalizing Influences on Secondary Education

and secondary education. Indeed, this kind of comment often accompanies proposals about education irrespective of whether the commentator favors or opposes an increase in federal action. Hanna, in proposing some system of national curriculum development, says,

> I see no need for changing the existing legislative provision for local and state responsibility for the schools. I am for federal financial support to the states to help equalize the states' ability to provide a minimum educational opportunity for all citizens. I support the principle that the control of the curriculum of our schools should be kept in the hands of the people, decentralized.[2]

The purpose here is not to support or criticize these often expressed positions concerning public education, but to examine the assumption that underlies these positions. The assumption is that public education is controlled by local governments under the conditions laid down by state governments. Is local educational government, in fact, dominant as far as the management and control of the public schools are concerned? Or are there other forces which play a major part in shaping the schools' destinies? Many people seem to take the answer to this question for granted. To them the "truth" is so self-evident, it needs little or no investigation. Local control has been, is, and should be the hallmark of a system of public education.

There are a few people, however, who question that local control is now an accurate characterization of our system. Campbell has pointed out what he calls the "folklore" which has grown up around the idea of local control.[3] More recently the State Superintendent of Public Instruction of Florida said,

> But what is local control today? Those who think that such control involves the absolute right of local persons to make decisions without reference to higher authority have accepted folklore as fact, for local control of this type is nonexistent today.[4]

Grodzins feels that it is impossible to designate a significant aspect of government which is solely local. He says,

---

[2] Paul R. Hanna, Professor of Education at Stanford University, "A National Curriculum Center: Threat or Promise?" paper presented at Harvard University, July 9, 1959 (Mimeographed.) For a shorter version see—Paul R. Hanna, "A National Curriculum Commission," *The NEA Journal*, XLIX (January, 1960), 25-28.
[3] Roald F. Campbell, "The Folklore of Local School Control," *The School Review*, LXVII (Spring, 1959), 1-16.
[4] Thomas D. Bailey, "The Folklore of Local Control," *The NEA Journal*, L (December, 1961), 42-43.

In the most local of functions—law enforcement or education, for example—the federal and state governments play important roles . . . from abattoirs and accounting through zoning and zoo administration, any governmental activity is almost certain to involve the influence if not the formal administration, of all three planes of the federal system.[5]

Against this background of comment and opinion, much of which is very insightful, the purposes of the studies reported here become significant and timely. If we are to consider a change in the traditional relationships between local, state, and national agencies in education, it behooves us to understand what is actually happening at each of these levels. If we are to deal effectively with the new programs operating at the national level, we must understand the impact these programs have on the schools.

The area of possible investigation is a large one and, for this reason, the investigation had to be delimited. The possible influences on the schools are numerous, ranging from various programs of categorical federal aid to recent critics without credentials who create crises in school systems by a variety of devious means. The decision was made to examine a number of discernible agencies, all national in scope, that have the power to influence by virtue of their authority, financial resources, or prestige. Even with these limitations, more than fifty nominations of various organizations were considered. These included governmental agencies, religious organizations, foundations, professional associations, accrediting bodies, business organizations, and others.

Further limitation occurred when it was decided that the primary purpose of a given agency must be related to education. The United States Chamber of Commerce, for example, even though it has an extensive program relating to educational issues, was not included in the final list.

National movements have affected colleges and universities in many ways, but such influences will not be examined in this monograph.[6] Both elementary and secondary schools have responded to national movements, and it is the investigation of the impact on the high schools that will be reported here.

---

[5]Morton T. Grodzins, "The Federal System," *Goals for Americans,* Report of the President's Commission on National Goals (New York: Prentice-Hall, 1960), p. 267.

[6]See: Homer D. Babbidge, Jr. and Robert M. Rosensweig, *The Federal Interest in Higher Education* (New York: McGraw-Hill Book Co., Inc., 1962).

4 Nationalizing Influences on Secondary Education

American high schools, because of their customary departmental structure, can be broken into more discrete elements than elementary schools. This leads to the assumptions that a teacher or department chairman in a high school is aware of the impact of new curriculum programs, and that a high school counselor or administrator is informed about the activities of nationwide testing programs. Therefore, the breadth of the study was reduced by considering only those influences related directly to high school programs.

At this point, the list included:

1. Professional educational organizations—such as the National Education Association and the American Association of School Administrators.
2. Regional accrediting bodies—the North Central Association in the Midwest.
3. The National Science Foundation—a quasi-governmental program at the federal level.
4. The National Defense Education Act of 1958—a broad federal program including support in specific areas, such as science, foreign language, mathematics, and guidance.
5. Foundations—such as Carnegie, Ford, and Kellogg.
6. Nationwide testing programs—the College Entrance Examination Board and the National Merit Scholarship program.
7. Organized special interest groups.

Depth interviews with school officials and teachers in seven Chicago area high schools enabled the team to decide on four major influences which then were studied by means of a questionnaire to the chief school officials of 240 Illinois high schools. The analysis made of the depth interviews is found in chapter two, and the results of the questionnaire study are reported in chapter seven.

The four programs found to be important in the case studies and incorporated in the questionnaire are:

1. The National Science Foundation
2. The National Merit Scholarship Program
3. The National Defense Education Act of 1958
4. The College Entrance Examination Board

In addition to measuring the impact of these four selected programs on the high schools of Illinois, it was decided to include a chapter on each of the programs to develop a background against which to view their impact. Chapter three grew out of a recent doctoral dissertation on the National Science Foundation.[7] Likewise, chapter four reports the results of some careful case studies on the effects of the National Merit Scholarship Program found in another dissertation.[8] Somewhat less extensive and comprehensive treatments of the NDEA and the College Entrance Examination Board are found in chapters five and six. While these four agencies were found to be the most influential in the pilot interviews, and are dealt with in some detail here, other organizations and programs are not without influence or effect. Indeed, further investigation of other nationalizing influences on elementary, secondary, and higher education should be undertaken. Illustrative of the further research needed is the study reported in chapter eight dealing with the relationship between nationalizing influences and independent secondary schools.

The major hypothesis of this monograph is that there has been a change in the character of American educational government toward decreasing independence for local school systems. This change has been brought about by the emergence of a variety of influences which exist at the national level. Two approaches have been used to test this hypothesis: (1) study of the movements themselves, and (2) examination of the impact of these forces on the local schools.

The detection of changes in institutions over a period of time is not an easy one. It will be seen in succeeding chapters that, in fact, the influences selected for study could have been influential only during the last ten years or a lesser period. Even though we are not concerned specifically with shifts and changes during the whole period in which our state systems of education have existed, an overview of the history of certain national activities in education is helpful. This overview also gives us the basis for categorizing the influences found on the contemporary scene.

An Historical Note

The concept of local control in education, that is, the management of the schools by boards elected from the immediate school community, is so imbedded in our educational framework that the ulti-

---

[7]Lloyd J. Mendelson, "The National Science Foundation and Educational Policy" (Unpublished Ph.D. dissertation, Department of Education, University of Chicago, 1962).

[8]Lorraine LaVigne, "Impact of the National Merit Scholarship Program on the Public High School" (Unpublished Ph.D. dissertation, Department of Education, University of Chicago, 1962).

mate source of authority and control, the state, is often obscured. When school patrons are asked who controls the schools, the overwhelming reply is that the local board of administration has this authority. Most parents are unaware that the state gives and can take away authority. The erroneous view that the state is usurper rather than the holder of legitimate power over education has considerable significance for those who contemplate the possibility of increased federal activity. Will of the United States Office of Education writes,

> Centralizing tendencies in administration strike at the very roots of laissez-faire concepts that have led many persons to believe that the local governments and private entities permitted to function within a state under constitutional and statutory law can do as much as they please without interference from State administrative agencies. Those who hold these concepts often challenge the rights of State administrative agencies to apply or enforce their rules. They see central administrative authority as the embodiment of all "isms" that are alien to democratic government.[9]

In this study, the state and local aspects of educational government are considered as representing one level of educational control. This level has been termed the state-local. Though this collapsing of two functional levels into one may do some injustice to the complex set of state and local relationships, it is justified from a legal point of view and it does enable national influences to be brought into sharper focus as they impinge upon state systems of education. The study then seeks to determine if the influences selected have caused a shift in the locus of decision making from the state-local to the national level.

National influences, especially those of the federal government, can be noted early in our nation's history. The land endowments for public schools accomplished through the federal Ordinances of 1785 and 1787 were looked upon as having great potential value. It was first thought that the income from these lands would in time entirely support the common schools. Later this idea had to be modified when it was seen how little yearly income these sources produced and how rapidly the population of the country was increasing. This early federal action, however, was a factor in the movement which resulted in the development of tax-supported and publicly controlled schools.

Land grants represent one type of federal support and influence which has continued to this date. It was the giving of very moderate

---
[9] Robert F. Will, "State Administrative Rulemaking," *School Life*, XLIV (April, 1962), 19-21.

resources in order to encourage much greater state and local effort in the support and development of schools. This type of support was directed to no particular kind of educational program; there were no strings attached other than that it be used for public schooling.

Another type of support came more than a half century after these early programs when in 1862 Congress provided for grants of public land to each state, this time to found colleges of agriculture and mechanical arts. In these instances, also, the actual financial return from the land grants was disappointing but they did constitute a higher level of support than was found in the previous Ordinances. The significance of the Morrill Act is that the support was directed to specific, rather narrowly defined kinds of education at the college level and that the results were seen in terms of this rather specific purpose. Ultimately, the grants were widely accepted and an institution providing the specified training was created in every state. In some instances the land grant was used to add to existing state universities; a few of the states gave the grant to private institutions already established within the state; and the remainder established separate agricultural and mechanical colleges. One analysis of the effects of the land grant program suggests that higher education in the United States was redirected into "at least one stream that had direction and force."[10] American higher education with its private, religious character in the first half of the Nineteenth Century was given a new dimension by this action of the Federal Government.

Would it be far-fetched to recognize the results of the Morrill Act in the terms of a greatly expanded and redirected system of higher education, but also in terms of great progress in agriculture and engineering over the last century? Does this type of federal support find present day expression in programs which aim for scientific supremacy? Without question, the success of these Nineteenth Century endeavors has given impetus to modern federal programs which strive to augment and shape the contributions of higher education to our culture and economy.

Toward the end of the Nineteenth Century another type of influence came into existence which did not originate from the federal government but from powerful organizations or "private government." These were the regional accrediting associations which developed along with the rise of the high school. The fact that they are regional does not destroy their national character because examination will

---

[10]Homer D. Babbidge, Jr. and Robert M. Rosensweig, *op. cit.*, p. 9.

show a great similarity among these accrediting associations resulting in part from the close communications which they maintain. In drawing upon the work of the National Education Association Committee of Ten in 1892 and the work of the Carnegie Foundation for the Advancement of Teaching, these accrediting associations were able to standardize the high school program to a remarkable extent. The Carnegie unit is as standard in secondary schools as classrooms and teachers. It may very well be argued that these agencies were responsible for the development of secondary education at or above certain required minimum levels. This influence is characterized as a kind of volunteer program directed toward a specific level of American education and which standardizes the educational program.

The magnitude of governmental forces playing upon secondary education can be seen when we look, for example, at the enactment by Congress of the Smith-Hughes vocational education bill in 1917. This gave aid to the states for agricultural, home economics, and industrial education and created a vast system of vocational education, secondary and local in character but national in scope and purpose.

Inherent in these federal programs, and for that matter inherent in the private associations, is the element of persuasion rather than of coercion. Conformity is not demanded by law or other types of pressure but rather inducements, represented by the availability of money, accreditation, or other rewards, constitute the means of standardization. Inducement of this sort must be very powerful for even the moderate amounts of money offered by the federal government seem to have had great results in terms of the common and unified character of the American high school. If anything, accreditation may have meant more than money.

More recently we have witnessed another type of federal program. The National Science Foundation, which may be termed quasi-governmental because nongovernmental groups participate in the program, and the National Defense Education Act make relatively large amounts of money available for specific programs. Perhaps it is too early to make a final judgment about these federal acts since they have been in existence for only twelve and four years respectively, but their brief existence is the very thing which makes possible an entry into the problem of determining how quickly and to what extent significant national influences can be felt. Apparently convinced of the efficacy of the support for science, foreign languages, and mathematics, other subject matter groups which have not been included in these acts are now pressing for inclusion. It is reported that teachers of English and of social studies feel that the method of financial inducement for educational change embodied in these acts is appropriate for them as well as for the sciences.

The last of the national influences to be noted are the external testing programs. These are not new as a type but the scope of their activity has broadened significantly in recent years. When the College Entrance Examination Board served only a few high schools and colleges in the East, little concern was manifested by school officials. When this program and the newer National Merit Scholarship program began to affect high schools all over the country, a very serious and hard look was given these programs by secondary school officials. Holt, as Director of the Joint Project on Testing, suggests that the effect of external testing programs upon the high school curriculum is a most serious threat. He concludes:

> In the United States, considerable responsibility for administering the schools is assumed by the local community. This insures that the school will meet local, as well as national, needs; it provides the people with the continuous challenge of taking part in the education of their children and youth. Anyone who has joined a group of citizens in preparing a statement of goals and purposes for a local school knows how much this does to keep the school *public* and the program pointed in the right direction. By sharing in forming policies, the citizens maintain a process essential to our democracy. Nowhere in the world have democracy and education been so closely identified. Large scale external testing programs may detrimentally impinge upon this relationship. There is evidence that this is occurring.[11]

This brief historical note does not, of course, do justice to the full panoply of forces which have played upon American education. This historical analysis, however, gives us a rough means of classifying these forces. There are five categories:

1. Federal programs which offer a low level of support to education on a broad scale, e.g., the land grants of 1785 and 1787.
2. Federal programs which offer a low to moderate level of support for specific programs or types of institutions, e.g., the Morrill Act.
3. Federal programs which offer a relatively high level of support for rigorously defined elements in specific subject matter areas, e.g., N.S.F., N.D.E.A.
4. Nongovernmental programs which directly affect high school

---

[11]Joint Committee on Testing, *Testing, Testing, Testing* (Washington, D. C.: American Association of School Administrators, Council of Chief State School Officers, and the National Association of Secondary-School Principals, 1962), pp. 27-28.

programs by means of accreditation, e.g., the North Central Association of Colleges and Secondary Schools.
5. Nongovernmental programs which indirectly affect high school programs by means of external testing, e.g., the College Entrance Examination Board and the National Merit Scholarship Program.

In reality, these programs are not so discrete and not so simply described as the categories suggest. They overlap and there are various combinations of interdependent influences. It is the purpose of the succeeding chapters to look at these programs in detail and to ascertain if some relationship can be seen between the kind of support and the degree of influence, between the character of the school community and the degree of influence, and among other variables.

The debate is now taking place relative to the possibility of large scale support by the federal government for total elementary and secondary public school programs. This represents another, *though untried,* type of national influence. If we can learn something from the types of influence already in existence, we may be in a position better to evaluate the proposed federal programs and thus to participate intelligently in the decision.

The Guiding Questions

The studies reported here were carried out to provide answers to two different kinds of questions. The prior question in any investigation is the one of description, and discussions of the development, operation and growth of the four national programs which are central to this monograph are provided. With an accurate and complete description of the phenomena of interest available it is possible to move to the question of analysis. Various chapters report studies which were concerned with the identification of two kinds of effects that follow from the operation of the national programs: (a) the standardization of secondary education, and (b) the shift in the locus of decision making in secondary education from the local-state to the national level.

Some definitions are in order. Standardization not only suggests that high school programs will tend to be alike but that they will be alike in those specifics to which a particular influence addresses itself. For example, if certain course content is changed in the same way in a number of high schools because this will help students better meet the demands of an external testing program, we would call this standardization. If, on the other hand, we find that the availability of funds through the National Defense Education Act promotes diversity in science and mathematics offerings, we would have to draw a different conclusion about the tendency for this kind of program to standardize.

The idea of a shift in decision making from the local-state to the national level may not be easy to demonstrate, but it may be helpful to understand that this refers to the source of authority for given decisions. If a school faculty suggests a certain curriculum change because they have observed a successful program developed by one of the influential national bodies, we feel this would represent a shift in the locus of authority. Then, too, if state officials make recommendations to local schools based on their knowledge of a program originating at the national level this would be a shift. In both instances, the impulse for change has come from a level other than the one making the decision. Complicating this analysis is the difficulty of knowing how much leeway the local decision makers have. There is a difference between a local board adopting an Advanced Placement program because they consider it educationally sound and because they were subjected to irresistible pressure. Probably no decision exists in pure tones of black or white, but even the existence of grey decisions leads us to consider the external forces which contribute to the decision.

The interview and questionnaire techniques developed for this study were designed to detect an increasing or changing pattern of external influences that impinge upon a given school system. Moreover, they were designed to determine how and to what extent the schools reacted to these external influences.

On the other hand, the three dissertations reported vary in design, but share a focus on national programs which are steadily increasing in size and importance to secondary schools. It has already been noted that these influences are offered to the three major groups in the school; teachers, students, and the school administration (including the board of education). Teachers are given opportunities for paid study through the National Science Foundation and the National Defense Education Act. Students are awarded scholarships and opportunities for desired college placement by means of the two external testing programs. The school administrations may obtain money for materials and facilities. The three groups taken as a whole are confronted with new and improved curricula.

For many people, including the authors of this monograph, it is difficult to talk about the ways in which schools are changing or should be changed without making value judgments stemming from strongly held beliefs. There are those who feel that the pattern of local control should be maintained at all costs and that any efforts of the federal government in support of education are dangerous. There are those who feel that the pattern of local control has kept the schools from making desirable progress and that the only way to make progress is to institute some pattern of federal support and perhaps of control. There are a number of positions between these two points of view. Adherents of the extreme positions may not be interested in objective findings about the complicated dynamics which now characterize the relationships among all the agencies interested in education. But an objective analysis of the relationships will do much to help the adherents of all positions to judge the merits of their positions concerning educational government. While this monograph is not directly concerned with value judgments about how our public schools should be governed, it is intended to throw some light upon what is happening to secondary schools at this point in the twentieth century.

A recent report from the United States Office of Education underscored the need for knowledge about the forces which affect education. In the reorganization of the Office of Education, an addition to the Office of Legislation and Program Planning is to be known as the Federal Programs Branch. Its function will be to survey the effects of various government programs on all levels of education.[12] It is to be hoped that this monograph will contribute to a fact finding effort which will supplement the need evident in this action of the Office of Education. Major decisions about federal aid to education; decisions to establish national curriculum agencies; in fact, any decision which has broad implications should be made on the basis of research and consistent with the basic values of the nation.

---

[12]"Reorganization of the Office of Education," *School Life*, XLIV (April, 1962), 16-17.

Exploratory Studies

Roald F. Campbell | Chapter 2

There appear to be a number of influences, in government and out of government, which are tending to nationalize our schools and colleges. This chapter reports one aspect of a larger investigation in which the nature and extent of these influences are being examined. In the first stage of the investigation it seemed desirable to identify a rather large range of these purported influences and to determine to what extent such influences were present and important in a number of public secondary schools. An attempt was made to answer the following questions: (1) To what extent are certain national influences found in selected secondary schools? (2) Do these influences appear to contribute to the standardization of educational programs? (3) Do these influences represent a shift in decision making from the local-state to the national level?

Seven secondary schools were selected and a case study was made in each of them. An attempt was made to secure schools that represented a considerable range in socio-economic and educational characteristics. The sample schools are described briefly in Table 1.

It will be noted that the schools are located in a large city, a middle-sized city, several suburban communities, and one rural and farm center. Some of these communities are essentially residential, others essentially industrial. The dominant social class in these communities ranges from upper middle to lower middle and upper lower. The enrollments in the high schools ranged from 700 to 4100.

After considerable examination of a wide variety of purported national influences, it was decided that the following would be used in this study: professional associations of teachers and administrators, the regional accrediting association, the Division of Scientific Personnel and Education of the National Science Foundation, the National Defense Education Act, the philanthropic foundations, the

TABLE 1

CHARACTERISTICS OF SECONDARY SCHOOLS IN WHICH CASE STUDIES WERE DONE

School	Type of Community	Social Class*	Enrollment
A	large city residential	middle, lower middle	4100
B	middle size city residential & industrial satellite	middle	3740
C	suburban residential	upper middle	1750
D	suburban residential	middle	1100
E	suburban residential & industrial	middle lower middle	3400
F	suburban industrial & residential	lower middle	2800
G	rural and farm center	lower middle, & upper lower	700

*Social class designations refer to predominant population group or groups as given in the *Suburban Fact Book*, published by the Northeastern Illinois Metropolitan Area Planning Commission, June, 1960.

College Entrance Examination Board, the National Merit Scholarship program, and a miscellaneous category called special interest groups. A structured interview guide in which pertinent questions regarding the presence of programs related to each of these influences was prepared.

In each school five to nine extended interviews were held with the people thought to know most about the possible impact of the various influences under study. In all cases interviews were held with the superintendent of schools, the principal, a guidance director, and a science instructor. In most cases, a director of instruction or an assistant principal and a mathematics instructor were also included. In some cases biology and foreign language instructors were also interviewed. Interview protocols were prepared for each school and became the data for this chapter.

Findings

The findings will be reported in terms of each of the eight purported national influences. With respect to professional associations, teachers and administrators were, without exception, members of national associations and the state affiliates of these groups. The American Association of School Administrators was generally thought to be the most important affiliation by superintendents, the National Association of Secondary School Principals by principals, the National Personnel and Guidance Association by guidance workers, and the National Council of Teachers of Mathematics and the National Science Teachers Association by mathematics and science teachers respectively.

It is interesting to note that each of the associations mentioned most frequently, except the one in guidance, is an affiliate of the National Education Association. The Parent Teacher Association was also mentioned frequently by superintendents, less frequently by other interviewees, as an important professional affiliation. In terms of participation in these associations, such as serving as officers and on important committees, suburban school personnel appeared to be the most active. Respondents in the large city school held membership but appeared to look to their own central administration for guidance more than they did to their professional associations.

There were some exceptions to exclusive membership and participation in NEA and its affiliated associations. Locals of the American Federation of Teachers were found in schools A, B, E, and F. These schools were in the two cities and in the two industrialized suburban communities. One science teacher also had membership in the American Physical Society, the membership of which is largely college instructors in the subject.

The Commission on Secondary Education of the North Central Association of Colleges and Secondary Schools has recently established some "approval" and some "progress" criteria. This new formulation was used as the basis for ascertaining the relevance of this organization to the high school. All seven schools were accredited by the North Central Association and this accreditation was looked upon as important by the respondents in each school. The principals of the schools were fully aware of the progress criteria and able to describe the degree to which their schools already met such criteria.

The importance assigned to the North Central Association varied by type of school. Again School A in the large city looked to its central office more than to an outside agency. In terms of the ratio of guidance workers to pupils, for instance, NCA standards were ignored. Schools B, C, D, and E serving upper middle and middle class populations for the most part, made it very clear that their practices exceeded NCA standards. At the same time administrators in some of these schools had used the threat of non-accreditation as one argument for the passage of levy elections. In Schools F and G serving lower middle and upper lower class populations, it was found that the North Central Association was of even greater assistance in convincing the communities that certain standards were desirable.

The superintendent of School F put it this way, "Our school is fully accredited and has remained so since 1907. We have always responded to the suggestions and directions received from North Central."

One might ask why a regional accrediting association was included as a national influence. Two reasons can be given. One, the North Central Association operates in nineteen states, a rather large segment of the nation. Two, the regional accrediting associations have a loose federation and many of their programs are similar in character. In effect these associations appear to be another national influence.

The National Science Foundation portion of this inquiry dealt chiefly with the fellowships provided for mathematics and science teachers and with the various curriculum programs supported by NSF money but directed by professors at selected universities. For instance, the Physical Science Study Committee was organized at the Massachusetts Institute of Technology and the School Mathematics Study Group was organized at Yale University, though the latter has now been moved, with its director, to Stanford University. Similar programs have been organized in biology and chemistry.[1]

All seven schools studied have had science or mathematics instructors in the summer or year-long institutes sponsored by NSF. In most cases several instructors in both science and mathematics had experienced this type of in-service training. In one school eight of the nine mathematics instructors and in another school seventeen of the eighteen mathematics instructors had been institute participants. Six of the seven schools made modifications in existing science and mathematics courses, added a new course, or adopted the entire physical science program as a result of this training.

In School A in the large city, science and mathematics instructors seemed to be less aware of the national curriculum programs, but the

---

[1] See: *The School Review*, LXX (Spring, 1962). The entire issue is devoted to description and discussion of the curriculum programs of NSF.

influence of the school Mathematics Study Group was apparent in the new mathematics course of study used in School A. The chairman of the mathematics department of School C in the upper middle class suburb remarked, "Whether you approve or not, you must try it out because of the pressures that are applied by the community." Clearly the patrons of School A and School C are responding quite differently to the same programs of the National Science Foundation.

Funds available through the National Defense Education Act had been used in all seven schools to purchase equipment or to remodel rooms for teaching science, mathematics, or foreign language. One science department chairman remarked, "NDEA has oiled the latch for getting science equipment." Three of the seven schools had built language laboratories and such laboratories were planned in two additional schools.

In four of the seven schools guidance personnel had attended summer or year-long institutes underwritten by NDEA and sponsored by various universities. Two schools had language instructors who attended foreign language institutes organized under similar auspices. The superintendent of School C said that NDEA was "intensely controlling, but the institutes are of decided value."

School A had increased the number of language instructors on its staff since 1958 and School B had expanded its language staff from four to ten teachers. Five schools increased their counseling staffs since the advent of NDEA and three schools augmented their testing programs as a result of NDEA stimulation. School A added a course in the introduction to college mathematics seemingly because of the influence of NDEA. All of these changes in a space of four years suggest that NDEA has been a pervasive and powerful influence on the programs in these schools.

The influence of the philanthropic foundations on schools was more difficult to determine. Three of the schools, A, C, and G, recognized no foundation influence. One of these was in the large city where there were several foundation sponsored programs, but their impact seemed to be chiefly on schools other than A. Respondents in Schools B and F recognized that the Conant studies were supported by the Carnegie Corporation and respondents in Schools B, E, and F recognized that the staff utilization studies of the NASSP were supported by Ford grants. Officials in School B were aware of Ford support of a Superior Talent Student program in which School B had participated with other NCA schools. Only in school F did a respondent offer knowledge of Ford support of the Midwest Airborne Television Program.

Clearly many respondents were unaware of the role played by foundations. This in spite of the fact that the Conant reports, the activities of Trump and associates and airborne television have had at least some influence on each of the schools. Apparently, many of the programs supported by foundations were identified with the personnel conducting these programs, and their foundation connection was not always perceived.

The College Entrance Examination Board program appeared to have affected all seven schools. C, D, E, and F were among the 1225 high schools in the nation applying for membership in 1959 but were not among the 50 schools selected for membership by CEEB at that time. School A in the large city and School G in the farm center community did not apply for membership. School B had membership in the American Council on Testing with headquarters at Iowa University, a kind of competing college entrance board.

All schools except G have used CEEB tests, but in School B the ACT examinations were favored. Three of the seven schools were already offering Advanced Placement courses. Respondents in G expressed the hope that they would have an Advanced Placement course within two years. Schools C, D, E, and F, even though not members of CEEB, have sent representatives to the meetings called by the Board.

The superintendent and a counselor in School C intimated that they were under some pressure to conform to CEEB programs. Said the counselor, "This is the door through which the kids are able to get into college, especially the Ivy-League colleges." And again, "We're forced to participate in this program. If we expect this school to maintain its high level of college enrollment we have to go along." Two other remarks seem pertinent. The director of instruction of School C said, "CEEB will make teachers more test conscious and less experimental." The principal of School E put it this way, "CEEB calls the shots and the schools have to jump." Perhaps CEEB has become a standardizing agency dominated by the 427 colleges and universities and the 165 high schools (admitted since 1959) which constitute its membership.

The National Merit Scholarship program was organized in 1955 and financed initially with grants from Ford and Carnegie Foundations. All seven schools in this study have been in the National Merit program from the beginning. In 1961 some 950 students in these seven schools took the qualifying examination. In the six years over which the program has operated, however, these schools have had but one "scholar" and he came from School C.

Exploratory Studies   19

Only one of the seven schools acknowledged strong community pressure to produce scholars in the National Merit competition. The counselor of School C in the upper middle class suburb said that they provided a coaching session one day each week to "help give our pupils the same advantage as some of the North Shore schools which have been doing this type of thing for many years." The superintendent indicated that the next school board election might hinge on the issue of doing better in the National Merit Scholarship program. One teacher in School F acknowledged that some coaching was provided National Merit competitors, but the other five schools apparently provided no coaching and felt no pressure to do so.

Respondents in Schools E and F indicated that the National Merit program had made teachers more conscious of their work and in School E physics had been placed in the junior instead of the senior year so as to help students who take the National Merit examinations. It may be that the extent of these examinations has prompted teachers to teach pupils to pass tests more than the respondents acknowledged. Respondents in Schools A and C objected to the plan followed by NMS in allocating some winners to each state. They felt that "competition is much more strenuous in Illinois than in some other states, hence some very able students are not being recognized."

Possible pressures imposed by special interest groups evoked little response from the interviewees. In fact, most respondents in six of the seven schools said they felt no such pressures. Only in School C did such pressures appear to be readily recognized. Even here the superintendent and the director of instruction appeared to have different views of the pressure. The latter said that one group threatened to get his job because of his refusal to permit "Operation Abolition" to be shown in the school. Later the superintendent acknowledged that "Minute Men" were active in the community. The director of instruction was also certain that other right wing groups were at work in the community.

Interestingly, "Operation Abolition" was promoted in School D by the Daughters of the American Revolution and in School E by the American Legion. Both groups conferred with school officials and agreed to withdraw the request. School F interviewees knew of a woman who had promoted the Christian Anti-Communist Crusade, but when she left the community the movement seemed to collapse.

Some schools were using instructional materials prepared by groups such as the American Banking Institute, the Council for

Economic Education, the Institute of Life Insurance, and the American Medical Association. The possible influences of these materials may not have been fully appreciated. Officials in some schools reported rapport between the school and such organizations as the American Legion, Veterans of Foreign Wars, and service clubs. The fact that the schools may reflect values very similar to the values held by certain of the pressure groups would account for the few pressures experienced. The breadth of this category may also have mitigated against receiving more insightful responses from the interviewees.

Conclusions

It is clear that interviewees in the seven schools saw many of the eight influences present in their respective schools. Moreover, in many cases specific changes in courses taught, in testing practices, and in community relationships attested to the impact of these influences.

National influences do seem to be affecting secondary schools. Professional associations, most of which are affiliated with the NEA, may provide a persistent party line for teachers and administrators but these associations are not strong innovative influences. The impact of accrediting associations is probably minor except for schools like F and G where as one official said, "The NCA, directly and indirectly raises the sights and goals of the school through establishing standards which influence the schools in a desirable direction." Philanthropic foundations probably affect all schools to some extent but this influence is often not recognized by school personnel. Pressures of special interest groups appeared to be mild but part of this impression may grow out of the lack of recognition of such pressures.

The strongest influences felt by the seven schools studied were undoubtedly the CEEB, a non-public organization; the National Science Foundation, a quasi-public program; and the NDEA, a public program. Incidentally, all other programs examined in this study were non-public in character. The three strongest programs, despite their difference in sponsorship, tend to reinforce each other. All give great impetus to strengthening the academic offerings of high schools.

The degree of the impact of these national forces seems to be related to the type of community in which the school is located. School A found in a middle class community of a large city seems to have been most successful in resisting national movements. In most instances the central administration of the school system was the reference point rather than a national program.

School C in an upper middle class suburb, on the other hand, was embroiled in every movement. School personnel often referred to community pressures but it should be noted that these community pressures reflected the national movements.

Our second question dealt with the possible standardization of school programs as a result of these national influences. There does appear to be a movement toward standardization. Even the minor influences including the professional associations, the foundations, the National Merit program, and the right wing groups are national groups and are calling for uniform programs across the nation.

But the evidence for standardization does not rest on such implications alone. A great many high schools are now using the examinations of the CEEB. Passing these examinations is important to students, parents, and teachers of our high schools. For some, these tests have become a major criterion of high school effectiveness.

Even more dramatic is the influence of the National Science Foundation. If our sample is at all indicative, many high school teachers have now been members of the institutes organized under the aegis of the National Science Foundation, have learned the new science and the new mathematics, and are now engaged in revising their own courses. Moreover, direction for such revision is readily at hand for concurrent with the institutes have been the study programs in physical science, mathematics, biology, and chemistry. This is curriculum revision at the national level, a program inconceivable to most school people before World War II.

The NDEA has augmented science and mathematics revision by providing money for equipment and plant modernization. But NDEA has gone further and supported institutes for foreign language teachers and guidance personnel similar to the institutes sponsored for science and mathematics teachers by the NSF. It seems clear that guidance in this country now means what NDEA says it means. At no other time in our history has money been available for teacher fellowships to provide a standardized program of training in this area of school service.

One other factor probably contributes to this standardization. With the increasing mobility of our population and national coverage of matters educational in mass media, people across the nation tend to become more and more alike. An upper middle class suburb near Chicago for instance, is much like an upper middle class suburb near New York, Cleveland, Detroit, or San Francisco. We strongly suspect that the influences surrounding School C in this sample would also be found in scores of schools similarly situated elsewhere.

We come now to our third question; the possible shift in the locus of decision making from the local-state to the national level. It will be recalled that the College Entrance Boards, the institute and curriculum programs of the National Science Foundation, and the National Defense Education Act appeared to be the strongest of the influences we examined both in the preceptions of the interviewees and in the actual changes in school practices reported. These three influences are products of the 1950's. The National Science Foundation was begun in 1950. The National Defense Education Act was passed first in 1958 and the College Entrance Examination Board expanded its membership to include high schools and set up three regional offices in 1959.

Two of the minor influences are also of recent origin. Foundations have increased in number and resources in the last decade and are channeling a sizeable proportion of their resources into the field of education. The National Merit Scholarship program was organized in 1955 and in 1959 opened its testing program to all high school seniors who wished to take it.

All five of these influences are national in character. All of these programs have tended to ignore the local-state approach to educational problems, long the dominant pattern in this country. To be sure, all of these new programs are voluntary; no school district and no state legislature must accede to them. But in practice almost every state accepted NDEA funds even though such acceptance required special legislation in some states. All seven of the sample schools, and most schools elsewhere, are meeting the requirements of and following the practices advocated by these new national bodies. Local boards of education have little choice when they are confronted by nation-wide programs characterized by scholarly insight, prestige, and money. We retain the forms of local-state government, but actually we have national government, much of it private government.

This shift from local-state to national policy making for education appears to be most pronounced in those school districts populated by middle and upper middle class people. These are the people who read, who communicate with their associates in similar communities, who are most mobile, who are upward striving, who wish their children to enter prestige colleges, who have little faith in professional educators, and who may look upon local-state decisions in education as provincial and out-dated. For some of these people reform in education is long overdue and only a great national but nongovernmental effort will do the job. For others, complete local autonomy in education is the cherished goal.

This discussion is not intended to deny that many of the reforms advocated by the national movements have been constructive ones. It may be that high schools did need to reconceive their academic offerings, scholars in the universities did need to work with high school instructors to bring content up-to-date, more money did need to be expended to provide adequate physical facilities. But the fact remains that the stimulation to do these things has come through national movements and these movements are tending to standardize education the country over.

These seven case studies lead us to make a few observations not necessarily related to the major questions we raised. We were impressed with the strong hierarchical orientation of School A in the large city. The movements which we have examined apparently have to affect the central office bureaucracy of a large city school district first and then be transmitted to the separate schools. A number of professional school people appear to be unaware of the nature and the strength of the national influences studied. This was most noticeable in terms of foundation programs and the pressures of special interest groups. School administrators often invoke one of these national influences, such as accreditation or NDEA assistance to help persuade reluctant board members and citizens to do more for the schools. Some of our interviewees were opposed to more federal aid, but saw it as inevitable. One said, "It will come and along with others I will line up at the trough."

These last observations and indeed our other conclusions need more study. Certainly the impact of each of the three major influences, College Board Programs, NSF institutes and curriculum programs, and NDEA, should be examined in many schools. Social class and type of community appear to be important variables in this impact and thus the relationship of these variables to the impact should be carefully assessed.

The National Science Foundation

Lloyd J. Mendelson

Chapter 3

A force has emerged on the educational scene during the past decade that is national in scope and unique in its mode of operation. The National Science Foundation (NSF) was established by statute in the Spring of 1950 as an independent agency in the executive branch of the Federal government.[1] The organization was given a broad mandate to strengthen basic research and education in the sciences. Endowed with considerable autonomy, NSF has brought its resources to bear on the improvement of science and mathematics instruction throughout the nation, particularly in the area of secondary education.

The National Science Foundation's budget for educational purposes has grown steadily from $1.5 million in 1952 to $85 million in 1962. Approximately $100 million has been appropriated for the current fiscal year, 1963.[2] Programs initiated and supported by the Foundation have extended into such areas as supplementary teacher training, curriculum improvement, fellowship grants, small college support, international science education, and a variety of activities directly affecting secondary school and undergraduate students.

It is the purpose of this chapter to explore the brief history of the National Science Foundation in order to understand how one kind of Federal agency has developed, an agency which appears to be having considerable influence on the direction of science and mathematics education in the secondary schools.

---

[1] "National Science Foundation Act of 1950," in U.S., *Statutes at Large*, LXIV, Part 1, 149. Cited hereafter as PL 81-507.

[2] U. S., Bureau of the Budget, *The Budget of the United States Government for the Fiscal Year Ending June 30, 1963* (Washington: U.S. Government Printing Office, 1962), p. 828.

Historical Background

Federal support of science is deeply rooted in American History. Since the founding of the Republic, the government has played an important role in the promotion of major science ventures, and reciprocally has benefited from the resulting scientific contributions.[3] At critical periods in our history, institutions have been created that have enhanced the role of scientists as advisors to the government. During World War II, however, the pattern of relations between the Federal government and science were altered radically. The social forces engendered during this period led to the movement to establish a government foundation on behalf of science.

Research expenditures during the war more than trebled so that by 1945 approximately a billion dollars per annum were obligated for scientific research, with the federal government having replaced industry as the chief source of such funds.[4] The accomplishments in applied science, highlighted by successes in such areas as atomic energy and medical research, led to recognition of the need for greater efforts in basic research. The operations of the Office of Scientific Research and Development (OSRD), the war-time Federal agency responsible for planning and coordinating research programs, had placed government subsidized scientists in a position of greater strength than ever before.[5] International tensions between the United States and the Soviet Union, which began to emerge during the war and have continued to the present, reflected the tie-in between national security and scientific research.

The idea of a government foundation on behalf of science was conceived during World War II, primarily as a means of lending Federal support to basic research in the postwar period. Practical impetus was given to this movement by a group of government scientists and legislators spearheaded by Vannevar Bush, Director of OSRD at the time. Bush's plan was projected in a report prepared at the request of President Roosevelt, entitled, "Science, The Endless

---

[3] See: A. Hunter Du Pree, *Science in the Federal Government* (Boston: The Belknap Press of Harvard University Press, 1957).

[4] U.S., Congress, Senate, Subcommittee on War Mobilization of the Committee on Military Affairs, *Legislative Proposals for the Promotion of Science, The Texts of Five Bills and Excerpts from Reports*, "The Government's Wartime Research and Development, Findings and Recommendations, from Report of Subcommittee on War Mobilization," 79th Cong., 1st Sess., 1945, 27-28.

[5] Vannevar Bush, *Modern Arms and Free Men* (New York: Simon and Schuster, 1949), p. 6.

Frontier."[6] This document contained the basic formulation for the program and structure of a National Science Foundation.

Through the efforts of Bush and certain legislators, particularly Senator Magnuson of Washington and Representative Mills of Arkansas, proposals to establish a government foundation were introduced in Congress in 1945. Comparable legislation also was initiated in the Senate about the same time by Senator Kilgore of West Virginia, chairman of the Senate Subcommittee on War Mobilization, and a proponent of an expanded Federal role in science.

While secondary to more dramatic issues confronting the nation in the postwar period, the need to divert Federal funds into an agency devoted to strengthening basic research efforts was recognized by civic, industrial, and labor leaders, as well as by the President and a substantial portion of the nation's legislators.[7] Nevertheless, the legislative battle to establish a Foundation was waged for five years, mainly because of differences on substantive issues among the forces in Congress, between Congress and the President, and to a limited extent, outside the government. These issues included the control and structure of the organization, patent policy, support for research in the social sciences, geographical distribution of funds, and security provisions. In 1947 Congress passed a Foundation bill, but it was pocket-vetoed by President Truman on advice of the Bureau of the Budget because control of the organization would have been too far removed from the President. Eventually the differences were reconciled, and passage of Foundation legislation was assured in the Spring of 1950 when economy objections in the House Rules Committee were overcome.

During this period, recognition must be accorded to the scientists who, sparked by the organizing efforts of the American Association for the Advancement of Science (AAAS), played a strategic role in working with legislators, lobbying on behalf of science legislation, and maintaining active interest among the scientific and academic communities.

Although the long-range implications of national science legislation for science education were not envisioned clearly at the time,

---

[6]Vannevar Bush, *Science, The Endless Frontier,* Report to the President on a Program for Postwar Scientific Research (Washington: U.S. Government Printing Office, 1945).

[7]U.S., Congress, Senate, Subcommittee on War Mobilization of the Committee on Military Affairs, *Science Legislation, Analytical Summary of Testimony Pursuant to SR 107 and SR 146,* 79th Cong., 1st Sess., 1945, 1-8.

there was sufficient awareness among legislators of the need to identify and insure a continuous flow of skilled manpower to meet basic research needs.[8] The various bills introduced to establish a National Science Foundation all provided for a scholarship and fellowship program to be administered in such a manner as to assure an adequate undergraduate and graduate education for the scientifically gifted. It was this feature of Foundation legislation that was especially attractive to educators. Conant regarded the scholarship and fellowship provisions as the most significant aspect of the proposed legislation and consistently stressed this point at congressional hearings.[9]

It would seem, therefore, that the educational provisions incorporated in the National Science Foundation Act were viewed as related to the basic research concept rather than in terms of providing major reconsideration of science education for all American youth.

The National Science Foundation Act

The basic document defining the purposes, functions, and structure of the Foundation is Public Law 81-507, the National Science Foundation Act of 1950. The Act, typical of much 20th century legislation, may be described as a broadly phrased but action oriented statute. The purposes of establishing the organization were stated in the preamble as follows: "To promote the progress of science; to advance the national health, prosperity, and welfare; to secure the national defense; and for other purposes."

The functions of the organization as delineated by the Act can be classified in four categories; (1) the promotion, support, and coordination of basic scientific research; (2) the awarding of scholarships and fellowships in the sciences, mathematics, and engineering; (3) the fostering of international scientific cooperation; and (4) the acquisition and dissemination of information regarding scientific and technical personnel.[10] Underscoring all of these functions was the authority given the Foundation to strengthen basic research and

---

[8] See: "Senate Report No. 9, March 3, 1949, To Accompany S. 247, a Bill to Create A National Science Foundation," U.S. *Code Congressional Service,* II, 1950, 2272.

[9] James B. Conant, "A National Science Foundation," Statement before the Committee on Interstate and Foreign Commerce, House of Representatives, March 7, 1947, as cited in *Science,* CV (March 21, 1947), 299.

[10] PL 81-507, Sec. 3. (a).

education in the sciences and to encourage the pursuit of a national policy for the promotion of these objectives.

Control of the organization was vested in a part-time National Science Board composed of twenty-four members and a Director, appointed by the President. In reality policy making functions are shared between the National Science Board and the Director, with the latter assuming the more important role in conjunction with his top echelon staff.

To administer the specific provisions of the Act, four divisions were created, the most important of which for purposes herein is the Division of Scientific Personnel and Education. This Division was given the responsibility of administering the scholarship and fellowship provisions and has become the source of all Foundation programs in support of education. The discretionary authority granted by the statute has enabled the Foundation to expand its activities in the educational field. The Act further provided for panels and commissions to assist the divisions in carrying out their functions in order to assure a wide representation in the determination of programs.

From time to time amendments to the Act of 1950 and executive orders of the President have defined further the scope of Foundation responsibility. For our purposes the important changes consisted of an amendment passed in 1953 which removed the $15 million appropriation ceiling and amendments passed in 1959 which were regarded as making explicit the Foundation's authority to support the varied educational programs.[11]

NSF Support for Education

As its initial venture, the Foundation launched a program of fellowship aid to graduate and postdoctoral students in the sciences in 1951 with grants totalling $1.5 million. Staff officials shortly thereafter proposed a series of additional programs on an experimental basis to meet the challenge of upgrading the quality of science education. The decade of the 1950's was characterized by the implementation of these proposals on an extended scale so that by the early 1960's the Foundation was supporting extensive programs in certain areas. These areas include the following: (1) financial aid for graduate students, advanced scholars, and teachers through seven

---

[11]"Amendments to National Science Foundation Act—H.R. 8284," in *U.S. Code Congressional and Administrative News*, II, 86th Cong., 2nd Sess., 1959, 2245.

30 Nationalizing Influences on Secondary Education

basic fellowship programs; (2) supplemental training of teachers of science, mathematics, and engineering through a system of institutes; (3) improvement in the subject matter of science and mathematics instruction, particularly at the secondary school level, through the financing of major curriculum studies; and (4) identification and motivation of talented high school and undergraduate science students through a variety of special programs.

Budget appropriations have grown steadily over the years to enable NSF to finance the more than thirty specific kinds of educational programs currently in existence. Table 2 illustrates the growth in Foundation expenditures for science education. Almost forty per cent

TABLE 2

OBLIGATIONS OF THE NATIONAL SCIENCE FOUNDATION IN SUPPORT OF EDUCATION IN THE SCIENCES, 1952-1962*

Fiscal Year	Total Obligations ($ million)	Obligations for Education ($ million)	Percentage for Education
1952	3.5	1.5	42.8
1953	4.8	1.4	29.2
1954	8.0	2.0	25.0
1955	12.3	2.1	17.1
1956	16.0	3.6	22.5
1957	40.0	14.4	36.0
1958	49.8	19.5	39.2
1959	132.9	62.0	46.7
1960	154.8	64.6	41.7
1961	176.0	70.0	39.7
1962	261.7	84.5	32.3
Totals	$859.8	$325.6	37.9%

*Sources: National Science Foundation and Bureau of the Budget.

of total NSF appropriations through fiscal year 1962, approximately $325 million, have been allocated to the improvement of science and mathematics education.

Table 2 reveals further that at certain periods appropriations were increased sharply so that the pattern of growth is more accurately viewed as one of relatively steady expansion for a few years interspersed with substantial increases in fiscal year 1957 and again in fiscal year 1959. The period of 1952-56 was characterized by the establishment of the fellowship programs, experimentation with institutes for the supplemental training of teachers, and other approaches on a minimal basis, such as traveling science libraries, visiting science teachers, support for science clubs, and conferences on science curricula.

Appropriation increases in 1957 resulted mainly from renewed congressional interest in the field of secondary school science education. This interest appeared to stem from Foundation studies that helped make appropriation subcomittees aware of Soviet educational and technical advances.[12] Accordingly, Congress earmarked a minimum funding level of $9.5 million that had to be spent for the training of high school science and mathematics teachers. The supplementary teacher institutes, therefore, were expanded during this period. In addition, the studies in curriculum improvement were launched, particularly the Physical Science Study Committee at the Massachusetts Institute of Technology; the fellowship programs were augmented; and several special projects in science education were initiated or continued.

TABLE 3

NATIONAL SCIENCE FOUNDATION ALLOCATION OF FUNDS FOR SCIENCE EDUCATION, FISCAL YEAR 1962*

Program	Allocation
Fellowships	$16,800,000
Institutes	40,900,000
Research Participation and Science Activities for Teachers	
Science Education for Undergraduate Students	
Instructional Equipment for Undergraduate Education	16,634,607
Science Education for Secondary School Students	
Public Understanding of Science	
Course Content Improvement	9,000,000
Scientific Personnel and Education Studies	1,149,700
Total	$84,484,507

*Source: National Science Foundation, Division of Scientific Personnel and Education.

[12] U.S., Congress, House, Subcommittee of the Committee on Appropriations. *Hearings, Independent Offices Appropriations for 1957*, 84th Cong., 2nd Sess., 1956, 509-60.

The tremendous increase in appropriations beginning in fiscal year 1959 and continuing to the present followed immediately the successful launching of the first earth satellite by the Soviet Union. Congress passed the National Defense Education Act of 1958 and tripled the National Science Foundation's budget for educational purposes. This phase has witnessed the flowering of Foundation support for the variety of programs in science education. The allocation of NSF funds for education in fiscal year 1962 is illustrated in Table 3.

Influences on Secondary Education

While NSF has been concerned with science education at all levels, major efforts so far have been devoted to the improvement of education in the high schools. The decision to concentrate on secondary education as the focal point was in accord with the thinking of Foundation officials as to primary needs.[13] Most of the basic programs supported by NSF, therefore, have been directed towards the status of high school science and mathematics instruction—improving the competencies of teachers, upgrading the content of subject matter taught, and enriching the experiences of science-oriented high school students.

The Teacher Institutes

The most heavily financed NSF program has been the series of institutes designed to improve the subject matter competencies of the nation's science and mathematics teachers. There are three major kinds of institutes, each one conforming to the work pattern of teachers.[14] Summer Institutes, the most extensively supported, provide four to twelve weeks study during the summer period. Academic Year Institutes provide full time study during the regular school session for a limited number of teachers who take a leave of absence. In-service Institutes provide part-time study opportunities in the evenings or on weekends for teachers who hold full time positions.

The institutes are conducted on a group basis, employing course materials and curricula designed to meet the needs of participating teachers. They are organized on a one to one basis between NSF and

---

[13]Alan T. Waterman, "Science in American Life and in the Schools," in *The High School in a New Era*, Francis S. Chase and Harold A. Anderson, eds. (Chicago: The University of Chicago Press, 1958), pp. 90-93.

[14]*Annual Report of the Division of Scientific Personnel and Education, Fiscal Year 1961*, (Washington: National Science Foundation, 1962), II, 16.

the host institution of higher education. Institutions desirous of conducting such a program submit proposals to NSF which in turn are screened by groups of panelists. (Approximately one-half of such proposals are acted upon favorably.) If accepted, the Foundation agrees to finance the projected direct costs and a portion of the indirect costs of the institute. The conduct of the institute then is under the control of the sponsoring institution, which submits a final report to the Foundation at the conclusion of the session. NSF staff members visit the institutes, hold annual evaluating conferences, and conduct workshops for institute directors. Needs for particular kinds of institutes are publicized each year in the program announcements of the Foundation which are circulated among the colleges and universities.

The institutes which began on an experimental basis in 1953 have had a phenomenal growth. They assumed a "mass character" by 1959 as a result of (1) Congress designating the minimum funding level that had to be spent on the training of secondary school teachers and (2) the substantial increase in NSF appropriations following the launching of Sputnik I. By 1961, Congress had increased the minimum funding level to $30 million.[15] NSF sponsored institutes in each of the past two years have reached an estimated 10-20 per cent of the nation's high school science and mathematics teachers. Approximately 85 per cent of all teachers participating in institute activities during this period have been secondary school teachers.[16]

Course Content Improvement

Foundation-supported programs in course content improvement are designed to update the subject matter of science and mathematics that is taught in the nation's classrooms. The basic approach has been to encourage research and teaching scholars to undertake projects of curriculum revision. These projects have been limited in design or extensive in scope. Whatever the magnitude, the Foundation supports the development of a promising new program and the instructional materials to carry it out. When the final product is reached after tryouts in selected schools, the new course or material is made available generally to schools and school systems that wish to adopt it.

The curriculum programs may be classified in three groups: (1) the major undertakings as exemplified by the Physical Science Study

---

[15] U.S., Bureau of the Budget, *The Budget of the United States Government for the Fiscal Year Ending June 30, 1962* (Washington: U.S. Government Printing Office, 1961), p. 186.

[16] Annual Report of the Division of Scientific Personnel and Education, *op. cit.*, II, 18-21.

Committee (PSSC), the School Mathematics Study Group (SMSG), and the Biological Science Curriculum Study (BSCS), to which sums in the millions of dollars have been allocated; (2) a considerable number of less extensive studies in many curricular fields (including psychology and anthropology) involving grants to university and scientific society personnel for the development of special techniques, methods, and specialized courses; and (3) the production of supplementary teaching aids, such as laboratory equipment, educational films and filmstrips, and experimental television programs.

Priority thus far has been given to the development of new courses and materials for secondary schools with more than 80 per cent of program expenditures having been directed to this level. Projects have been underway, however, at both the college and elementary school levels with a major science study program currently underway in the grade schools.

With regard to the major curriculum studies in mathematics, physics, biology, and chemistry, the Foundation has turned primarily to outstanding university scholars in the particular subject fields to develop and conduct the curriculum projects.[17] Control of the steering committees are in the hands of the university subject specialists. Secondary school teachers are brought into the particular program early, a few at the policy level, but assume a more important function in the writing and trying out of the material. Since the adoption of this general approach with PSSC in 1956, there is indication that NSF is modifying its subject specialist orientation to the extent of involving more science educators and school administrators in its curriculum activities.

By supporting a spiraling method of experimentation, the Foundation helps build a nation-wide commitment and desire to use the new courses. The spiraling effect involves an increasing number of persons—researchers, teachers, pupils—in each developmental phase of the study until the course is considered ready for general availability. During this period, which may last from two to four years, the new curriculum receives tryouts throughout the country, is reported in the professional journals, and acquires status in the eyes of the profession. NSF further dovetails its support of the curriculum studies with the Institute program so that teachers included in the experimental courses are given periods of in-service preparation.

[17]For an up-to-date description and analysis of the National Science Foundation's major programs in course content improvement, see: *The School Review*, LXX (Spring, 1962). Entire issue.

Direct Support for High School Students

The National Science Foundation has provided many different kinds of support over the years to stimulate the scientific capabilities of high school students. In general, these programs have attempted to interest students broadly in science and to provide enriched educational opportunities for students who have exhibited special talent. These programs are conducted specifically by universities, colleges, scientific societies, research organizations, and other groups.

NSF aided Science Clubs and Science Career information with a grant as far back as 1953 to Science Service, a nonprofit organization which provides direction to Science Clubs of America. NSF also supported Traveling Science Demonstration Lectures around the country over a five-year period. Ongoing programs include such activities as Traveling Science Libraries, Visiting Scientists to Secondary Schools, State Academies and local Academies of Science projects (Junior Academies of Science), and special Science Education Training for Secondary School Students.

The Foundation currently is stressing the development of special opportunities for the talented high school student through two programs, Summer Science Training for Secondary School Students and the Cooperative College-School Science Program.[18] Under these programs, high-ability students are given an opportunity for advanced study and research experience under competent scientists. The Cooperative College-School Program, a recent innovation, is designed to involve both high school teachers and their students in joint activity in order to have a greater effect on the participating schools.[19]

Fellowships

The granting of fellowships is the oldest of the Foundation-supported activities, and is regarded as an investment in the future of individuals with high scientific potential. As such, these programs retain a great deal of selectivity. Initially, NSF granted fellowships through competitive examination to meritorious graduate students and postdoctoral scholars in the sciences for research purposes. As additional needs became evident to the academic community, the Foundation instituted new fellowship programs, so that this type of support is now regarded as a means of improving the quality of in-

---

[18] Annual Report of the Division of Scientific Personnel and Education, *op. cit.*, II, 34-36.
[19] *Ibid.*, II, 35.

struction at the secondary school and college levels and of bolstering the faculties at less favored institutions of higher education. Conversely, Foundation officials have not seen fit to institute a scholarship program although authority to do so was granted expressly in the Act of 1950.

The Summer Fellowship Program for Secondary School Teachers of Science and Mathematics was started in 1959 to enable outstanding high school teachers to pursue advanced degree requirements through a special program of one to three summer's duration. Although there is some overlapping with the Institute program, the Summer Fellowships are designed primarily for teachers who plan long-range individualized programs of advanced study. As with the institutes, the fellowship provides a favorable weekly stipend plus dependency allotments, tuition and fees, and travel allowances. During a three-year period from 1959-1961, some 1450 fellowship awards were granted under the Summer Program.[20]

The Process of Educational Policy Making

During the course of implementing the broad provisions of the Act of 1950, NSF not only has influenced the direction of secondary school science and mathematics, it has also been thrust into a position of developing educational policy at the national level.[21] Through the astute abilities of its officials, the judicious use of its resources, and because of the peculiar relationship of the Federal Government to education, NSF has developed policies and programs to improve science education on a nation-wide scale. With the consistent encouragement of the Congress, the Foundation has emerged as a potent force in the educational arena.

The role of the Foundation in educational policy making stems: (1) from its position in the expanding Federal establishment for science, and (2) from the nature of the relationships with its major reference groups. The elaborate, although somewhat diffuse Federal science structure consists of various operating agencies and advisory groups in the executive branch of the government. At the operational level there are the special agencies, such as the National Aeronautics and Space Administration (NASA), the Atomic Energy Commission

---

[20]*Ibid.*, II, 2-4.

[21]For an extended treatment of this topic, see Lloyd J. Mendelson, "The National Science Foundation and Educational Policy" (unpublished Ph.D. dissertation, Department of Education, University of Chicago, 1962), pp. 102-14.

(AEC), and the National Science Foundation, as well as the various departments in the executive branch that engage in science activities to varying extents. At the advisory level to the President are the Federal Council of Science (composed of Federal agency representation), the President's Science Advisory Committee (composed of nongovernmental scientists), and the newly-created Office of Science and Technology to coordinate Federal agency work and to help formulate Federal science policy. Federal science activities are buttressed by two standing committees in the Congress, the House Committee on Science and Astronautics and the Senate Committee on Aeronautics and Space.

The National Science Foundation with its primary functions of supporting basic research and education in the sciences, occupies an integral position in the Federal scheme. In addition to being an operating agency within its own right, it serves in an advisory capacity to the President and its officials are represented on or have contributed to other advisory groups. To cite one example, in 1959 an important policy report issued by the President's Science Advisory Committee contained recommendations for strengthening science education which paralleled NSF supported programs in teacher training, curriculum revision, and encouragement of high-ability students. Three of the nine members of the panel that prepared the report were or had been associated with NSF in some capacity.[22]

The National Science Foundation has turned primarily to the academic community and to associated professional societies to determine basic needs and to help develop programs for improving the quality of science education. Foundation-supported programs have originated through formal and informal contact between Foundation officials and academic specialists. NSF funds in the main have filtered through the nation's colleges and universities, and to some extent, the professional science societies. To maintain a flow of ideas between the Foundation and its major clientele, the Division of Scientific Personnel brings in scientists from the universities on a rotating basis to serve as section heads of the basic program areas served by the Division.

In 1957, the Foundation and the U. S. Office of Education reached agreement with regard to primary contact sources in the area of science education. NSF would continue to work primarily through the organized scientific community and the institutions of higher educa-

---

[22]President's Science Advisory Committee, *Education for the Age of Science*, A Report to the President (Washington: The White House, 1959), pp. 30-36.

tion, while the Office of Education would continue to work through State Departments of Education and the educational community.[23] NSF, therefore, has not relied on developing relationships with the educational community and practicing school administrators. At the national level, however, the Foundation and the Office of Education engage in various cooperative activities, such as budget preparation, exchange of information, technical assistance, and jointly financed projects.

Congress, or more specifically, its appropriation and science committees, constitutes the other reference group of significance to the Foundation. Through the appropriation seeking mechanisms, the Foundation interprets and justifies its educational policies and programs. At the annual sub-committee hearings, the educational activities of the organization are reviewed, the effect of particular programs are scrutinized closely, and areas of concentration may be suggested by committee members. On occasion, a decision affecting directly the course of Foundation support may emanate from such hearings, such as the aforementioned minimum funding for high school science teachers. In one instance, congressional committees brought strong pressure to bear on the Director of the Foundation to revoke a fellowship award that had been granted to a graduate student at the University of Illinois because of a loyalty question.[24]

In the main, however, Congress has given its stamp of approval to the programs and policies of the Foundation, and has consistently supported its growth.

Conclusions and Implications

The unique place of the National Science Foundation in education can be understood in terms of its dual function as an instrument of national science policy and as an instrument of Federal policy in education. In response to the scientific advances in the past twenty years and the demands of national security, the elaborate Federal establishment for science has arisen. The National Science Foundation not only is an integral part of this Federal pattern, but its activities in science education are perceived as an essential element in the furthering of national science policy.

---

[23]*Annual Report of the Division of Scientific Personnel and Education to the Director, Fiscal Year 1958* (Washington: National Science Foundation, 1958), p. 56.

[24]See *Champaign-Urbana Courier,* June 29, 1961, 4. Also *Chicago Sun Times,* June 22, 1961, 11.

The National Science Foundation 39

The tie-in between the Foundation and the structures for science in both the executive and legislative branches of the Federal Government has resulted in smooth lines of communication between the organization and key sources for the acquisition of appropriations. In other words, it has been easier to accomplish certain educational improvements in the name of science than in the name of education.

The history of Federal action in education reveals that Federal interest has found expression largely in particular or specialized areas.[25] Federal educational activities further are diffused among many departments and agencies in addition to the Office of Education. The absence of a comprehensive Federal policy in education and a strong centralized agency for administering such a policy, if there was one, in effect, have made possible the development of alternative structural forces. These forces may grow in influence over a period of time under particular political and social conditions.

Such has been the case with the National Science Foundation and its impact on the educational scene. It is no accident that NSF has become, in effect, another Office of Education. Since 1958, two agencies for education have been recognized at the Federal level in the annual education messages of both Presidents Eisenhower and Kennedy.[26] Moreover, in the areas of science and mathematics education, it seems clear that NSF has become a greater force for educational change than the Office of Education.[27]

What are some implications of this trend? Has this extended Federal aid resulted in greater Federal control? Part of the answer is contained in the way NSF has functioned. The organization has brought its resources to bear on all aspects of science education, particularly at the secondary school level. With a sensitive ear towards possible accusations of undue control, NSF has stimulated local insti-

---

[25]Hollis P. Allen, *The Federal Government and Education,* The Original and Complete Study of Education for the Hoover Commission Task Force on Public Welfare (New York: McGraw-Hill Book Company, Inc., 1950), p. 333.

[26]See, for example, U.S., *Congressional Record,* "Message of the President of the United States—1958 Budget," 85th Cong., 2nd Sess., 1958, CIV, Part 1, 396.

[27]To cite one example, important experimental programs for curriculum improvement in mathematics are being conducted in six university and college centers. By far, the most extensive project in terms of funds allocated, geographical scope, and grade coverage is the SMSG program at Stanford (formerly at Yale). This project has been termed, "the largest united effort for improvement in the history of mathematics education." See Kenneth E. Brown, "The Drive to Improve School Mathematics," *The Revolution in School Mathematics* (Washington: National Council of Teachers of Mathematics, 1961), pp. 16-17. Mr. Brown is specialist for mathematics education in the U.S. Office of Education.

tutions and communities to develop new and imaginitive proposals while standing ready and eager to finance worthwhile projects.[28]

NSF has made its efforts felt on science education by projecting itself in many ways on varied fronts. By involving hundreds of scientists, scholars, and teachers in the determination of programs, the Foundation has attempted to insure an effective and diverse representation. Chase has expressed the point of view that the type of support rendered to the major curriculum studies minimizes the danger of Federal control and the growth of Federal bureaucracy.[29]

Nonetheless, it would be naive to assume that any agency or foundation, governmental or nongovernmental, which has considerable financial resources, does not exercise control in the realm of decision-making. The National Science Foundation by adopting a policy of lending support to university scholars and professional scientists has greatly strengthened the role of these groups in effecting educational change. Extensive Foundation support for major curriculum projects raises the question of whether we are witnessing a trend towards elements of a national curriculum with science and mathematics in the vanguard. It would seem likely that an increasing number of school systems will become a part of this movement if they wish to keep abreast of current developments. It would behoove school administrators and boards of education to be aware of this trend and to consider seriously its implications for their schools.

---

[28]"National Science Foundation Upgrades Teaching of Science," *Nation's Schools,* LXV (February, 1960), 69-70.

[29]Francis S. Chase, "Some Effects of Current Curriculum Projects on Educational Policy and Practice," *The School Review,* LXX (Spring, 1962), 145.

The National Merit Scholarship Program

Lorraine LaVigne

Chapter 4

What impact do national educational programs have on local educational institutions? A partial answer to this question can be found by selecting and studying one program which is national in scope yet local in application, the National Merit Scholarship Program. The sponsors of this program, in recognizing the national need for scholarships, assumed, in 1955, the financial burden of supporting a nationwide scholarship program. In doing so, they employed external examinations[1] to award scholarships to students throughout the nation. The Corporation also recognized the high school as the vital link between the stated goals of its program and the attainment of those goals. This chapter is based on a recent study which confined itself to the specific question: What impact has the National Merit Scholarship Program had on the public high school?[2]

Background and Problem

The National Merit Scholarship Program, financed by grants from the Ford Foundation, the Carnegie Corporation, and other donors, has granted nearly 6,000 scholarships having an estimated value of $29.5 million. The program functions in the following manner:

> The National Merit Scholarship Program is a nationwide cooperative program of assistance to students of exceptional ability and to

---

[1] The term "external examinations" is used, with slight modification, within the framework proposed by Tompkins in an editorial, "External Tests and the Schools," *The Clearing House*, XXXV (May, 1961), 515. External examinations are defined as those examinations offered to the school by national, regional, or state agencies for use by the agent primarily, and the school secondarily.

[2] Lorraine LaVigne, "Impact of the National Merit Scholarship Program on the Public High School" (Unpublished Ph.D. dissertation, Department of Education, University of Chicago, 1962).

the colleges they select. It is the largest independent scholarship program in the history of American education. Through this program, the country discovers its highly talented young people—wherever they are—and helps to prepare these exceptional young Americans to be better citizens and more effective contributors to the progress of business, industry, science, government, and the professions.

The National Merit Scholarship Corporation, which directs this program, is an independent nonprofit corporation devoted solely to scholarship activities. Its major goals are to identify students of unusual ability and to encourage them to attend college by providing the incentive of public recognition and by helping to eliminate financial barriers.

The National Merit Scholarship Corporation handles all phases of scholarship work from the selection of candidates to every detail of scholarship administration. It offers without charge an advisory service for scholarship sponsors and works with sponsors of scholarship programs both within and outside the Merit framework.

Corporations, foundations, associations, and individuals interested in the aims and methods of the National Merit Scholarship Corporation are invited to offer through its facilities sponsored Merit Programs. All costs of administration of the National Merit Scholarship Corporation, including the nationwide search for highly able students, are met from funds already available for that purpose. Every dollar received is used in its entirety for the students and their colleges.[3]

Although the National Merit Scholarship Program has been in existence since 1955, it is evident that consideration is still being given to federal support of a nationwide scholarship program. Numerous bills have been introduced in the United States Congress. Recently President Kennedy stated, "We must assure ourselves that every young person who has the ability to pursue a program of higher education will be able to do so if he chooses, regardless of his financial means."[4] The President's message, in explaining operational details, indicated that candidates would be selected on the basis of ability as determined competitively.

In his State of the Union Message to the Second Session of the 87th Congress, President Kennedy said:

I shall also recommend bills to improve educational quality, to stimulate the arts, and, at the college level, to provide Federal loans

---

[3]National Merit Scholarship Corporation, *Semifinalists in the Merit Program*, (Evanston, Illinois: National Merit Scholarship Corporation, 1961), p. i.

[4]U. S., Congress, House, *American Education. Message from the President of the United States Relative to American Education*, 87th Cong., 1st Sess., Document No. 92, February 20, 1961 (Washington: U. S. Government Printing Office, 1961), 4.

for the construction of academic facilities and federally financed scholarships.[5]

It is worthy of note that two national scholarship programs, one in existence, the National Merit Program, and one defeated Federal proposal employ or would have employed external tests to determine the awarding of scholarships to able students in need of financial assistance. In the National Merit Scholarship Program, test scores, although not the only evidence taken into account by the selection committee, are of primary importance in the selection of National Merit Scholars. The National Merit Scholarship Program, in using tests to determine Semifinalists and Finalists, has become a major factor in the external testing movement.

In brief, the National Merit Scholarship Program begins with the National Merit Scholarship Qualifying Test which is given to second semester juniors and first semester seniors in public, independent, and parochial secondary schools. The highest scorers in each state become Semifinalists. These Semifinalists take a second examination and provide the National Merit Scholarship Corporation with certain biographical and financial information about themselves. The results of the second test determine those who qualify as Finalists and are eligible to become Merit Scholars. A committee of evaluators makes the final selection of the Merit Scholars on the basis of test scores, high school grades, accomplishments outside the classroom, extra-curricular activities, school endorsements, and similar information submitted by the students and their schools. The Scholars are free to attend the colleges of their choice, and most of the scholarships are accompanied by a supplementary grant to the selected college. The Corporation has recognized that "Tuition seldom covers the cost of education."[6]

Methodology

This study of the impact of the National Merit Scholarship Program on the public high school employed the case study method, thus allowing for a detailed study of a limited number of high schools. The data, as collected, were subsequently converted into individual case study reports. These cases were then analyzed quantitatively and qualitatively to discover forms of impact and the relationship of

---

[5]U. S., Congress, *Congressional Record*, 87th Cong., 2nd Sess., CVIII, No. 2 (Washington: U. S. Government Printing Office, 1962), 51.
[6]National Merit Scholarship Corporation, *Merit Scholarships: The Programs; The Sponsors; The Scholars* (Evanston, Illinois: National Merit Scholarship Corporation, 1959), p. 7.

44 Nationalizing Influences on Secondary Education

these forms to selected variables. A pilot study allowed for formulation of hypotheses, construction of an interview schedule, testing of the instrument, and revision based on the pilot study findings. A decision to interview administrators, guidance personnel, and teachers directed the construction of the interview schedule. The study focused on the following hypotheses: assuming that the National Merit Scholarship Program has had an impact on the public high school, the forms of this impact are discernible and related to:

1. the rural-urban status of the community in which the high school is located,
2. the socio-economic class level of the inhabitants of the community,
3. the policies and procedures of the local high school.

The relationship between the socio-economic class of the community inhabitants and the level of success attained in the National Merit Scholarship Program was also subjected to critical study.[7]

Only high schools participating in the National Merit Scholarship Program were selected as sample schools. Only schools where the personnel indicated a willingness to cooperate in the study could be used. It was also essential to select schools located in rural, suburban, and urban communities which could be positively identified as representative of one or more of Warner's five levels of socio-economic class.[8] The selection of sample schools was limited by accessibility of schools in terms of distance to be traveled and time available to one investigator.

A representative sample composed of eighteen high schools was considered to be of sufficient size to supply essential data. Applying recent census percentages,[9] twelve of the sample schools were located in urban-suburban communities.

The dependent and independent variables consisted of qualitative and quantitative data relevant to the National Merit Scholarship Program. The forms of impact, qualitative in nature, were treated as

---

[7]Participants in the National Merit Scholarship Program can attain the status of: Letter of Commendation Winner; Semifinalist; Finalist; and Scholar.

[8]W. Lloyd Warner, *et al.*, *Social Class in America* (New York: Harper & Bros., 1960).

[9]For the United States in general, 69.9 per cent of the population is urban and 30.1 per cent rural. See: U. S., Bureau of the Census, *U. S. Census Population 1960*. Number of Individuals. United States Summary Final Report PC (1) 1A (Washington, D.C.: U. S. Government Printing Office, 1961).

the dependent variables. The data descriptive of the schools were collected in quantitative form and were treated as the independent variables. To quantify the qualitative data, a coding system was developed.[10] As interview responses were read and analyzed, major categories were formed. These categories, which later provided an outline form of the impact, were determined by the investigator, but to insure coder congruence, the interview responses were coded by two independent coders in addition to the investigator. This coding provided an outline form for the verbal reporting of the impact and a mass of quantitative data which was conveniently registered on IBM cards for future statistical computations.

The hypotheses, as proposed, guided the collection of the quantitative data which were treated as the independent variables. The hypotheses also included the concept of relationship. To obtain an estimate of the strength of the relationships between selected variables, coefficients of correlation were computed. After the relevant data had been registered on IBM cards, the computations were performed by machine following the Univac Program.[11]

Findings

Rating

The study revealed that the impact of the National Merit Scholarship Program had assumed seven general forms, the first being that of rating of schools. Respondents in thirteen of the eighteen schools reported that one of the most well-known results of National Merit participation was the rating of high schools by patrons of the school district. This rating process converted the program into an external measuring device which was used in an attempt to determine the quality of the high schools. This index of excellence was employed by board members, lay groups, and top administrators, regardless of the background of the students in attendance at the school being rated. Schools which had not experienced rating were aware of this use in other school districts.

John Stalnaker, President of the National Merit Scholarship Corporation, issued a warning in regard to this tendency to rate schools on the basis of National Merit success. Mr. Stalnaker stated:

---

[10] For a discussion of qualitative and code analysis, see: William J. Goode and Paul K. Hatt, *Methods in Social Research* (New York: McGraw-Hill Book Co., Inc., 1952), ch. xix.

[11] Tests for significance at the .05 level were employed. Only correlations significant at this level are reported.

> The quality or effectiveness of education within a state or within any school cannot be judged properly by the number of students in a state or in a school who are named Semifinalists. First, the number of Semifinalists in each state is determined through a representational system based upon the number of high school graduates in each state. Second, many factors can influence the number of Semifinalists in a particular school. For example, the attitude of a student's family toward educational achievement, the level of a community's support of its schools, and the purposes of the school are important. Other influences are the distribution of the population throughout the state, the size of the school, the native intelligence of its top students, and the nature of the community where the school is located . . . It is for the preceding reasons that the National Merit Scholarship Corporation considers comparison of schools on number of Semifinalists in each as unwarranted and unwise . . .[12]

Despite the efforts of Mr. Stalnaker, rating has continued in various communities and in the press. An editorial which appeared in a metropolitan newspaper had this to say:

> One index of the excellence of the nation's high schools is found in the annual award of National Merit scholarships. On the basis of this year's showings, congratulations are due the secondary schools in Chicago, its suburbs, and many other communities in the state.
>
> Chicago, which last year had 11 on the list, this year placed 17. The suburbs rose from 30 to 31—with Evanston and New Trier once more out in front with 5 and 4 respectively. Downstate had 15 winners last year, 19 this year. And the state as a whole, with 67 winners out of about 1,000 for the nation, scored its highest mark ever.[13]

Holt, in his extensive study of external testing, asked, "Will the community tend to appraise the effectiveness of a school by the number of national scholarship winners?"[14] According to the findings of this study, a correlation coefficient of .67 was obtained when the relationship between type of community and rating on the basis of National Merit results was tested. Communities which were classified as urban or suburban displayed a greater tendency to rate their

---

[12]National Merit Scholarship Corporation, *Semifinalists in the Merit Program*, p. iii.

[13]*Chicago Daily News*, April 27, 1961, 14.

[14]Charles C. Holt, "A Joint Committee Studies External Testing Programs," *Educational Leadership*, XVIII (January, 1961), 229.

schools on the basis of National Merit results than did rural and semi-rural communities.

In addition, a brochure published by the American College Testing Program reflected the extension of this rating to new programs. The following statement was issued by the ACT Program.

> The group results for an individual high school are kept strictly confidential and are available only to the high school itself. No lists of high scoring students are published. Everything possible has been done to prevent use of test results in published school-to-school or state-to-state comparisons.[15]

A controversial point appears here since one of the impact forms of the National Merit Scholarship Program was reported to be its key position in relation to the obtaining of other scholarships on the basis of high National Merit achievement. If National Merit publicity were reduced or eliminated, the extent of its influence on the winning of other scholarships would, most likely, decline. The extensive publicity may account to some degree for the rating of schools, but without publicity, the goals of the Corporation would not be so readily accomplished.

Preparation of Students

Since some schools were rated on the basis of National Merit results, various activities were designed by school personnel to "produce" Scholars. This seeking of methods designed to "produce" Scholars varied from school to school and had an effect on the curriculum, if curriculum is defined as all the experiences pupils have while under the direction of the school. However, a direct cause and effect relationship between the National Merit Scholarship Qualifying Test and the formal curricular offerings of the high schools could not be determined. It appeared that in discussing the National Merit Scholarship Qualifying Test respondents could not separate it completely from other college entrance and standardized examinations.

The types of assistance provided for students who were about to participate in the National Merit Scholarship Program include: train-

---

[15]The American College Testing Program, *ACT Information for Secondary School Educators* (Iowa City: The American College Testing Program, Inc., 1961/62), p. 11.

ing in test techniques, advanced placement classes,[16] review, or coaching classes,[17] using selected tests similar in form and content area for guidance and test practice purposes.[18]

When the first form of impact, the tendency to rate schools on the basis of National Merit results, and the second form, the use of various coaching methods designed to produce Scholars, were tested for strength of relationship between them, a correlation coefficient of .51 was found. This indicated that schools which were rated according to National Merit results employed various methods to produce Scholars over and above the regular offerings of the school. A correlation coefficient of .62 was found between type of community and use of various methods designed to produce Scholars. That is, the

---

[16]Stalnaker, in discussing curriculum planning and scholarship testing stated:
"You are aware of the advanced standing courses now being offered in some of our high schools. While given by a relatively small proportion of our secondary schools, these courses are having an influence on the other students and on all schools. In this case, the secondary school teaches with a specific test in a defined subject matter in mind. The students must develop explicit proficiency and knowledge in order to pass a test, ... The scholarship test of application cannot go so far because too few schools offer such courses. It must limit itself to the subjects considered fundamental by virtually all schools. In this way, it does not influence the curriculum but follows the pattern common to all schools."

John Stalnaker, "Implications of Curriculum Planning for Scholarship Testing," *Curriculum Planning to Meet Tomorrow's Needs,* 24th Educational Conference Educational Records Bureau (Washington: American Council on Education, 1960), p. 114.

[17]In a technical report published for counselors and school administrators, it was stated that "while the coachability of the National Merit Scholarship Qualifying Test itself has not been studied empirically, it is likely that, because of the nature of the National Merit Scholarship Qualifying Test, the only 'coaching' that could be more than minimally effective would require thorough grounding in broad skills of criticism and analysis, i.e., broad academic instruction." See: *National Merit Scholarship Qualifying Test Technical Report for Counselors and School Administrators* (Chicago: Science Research Associates, 1960), p. 23.

[18]A reviewer of tests finds it curious that the National Merit Scholarship Qualifying Test intended to identify students having high potential for college success should be so similar in design and content to a test which is intended as a measure of growth from grade 9 to grade 12. This reviewer said:

"Whatever the considerations that argue for a high degree of similarity in instruments intended for such apparently diverse purposes, it would be unfortunate if schools, in their zeal to have students do well on the scholarship examination, were influenced by the similarity to use Iowa Tests of Educational Development as, in effect, a warm-up or coaching exercise for the National Merit Scholarship Qualifying Test."

See: Roger T. Lennon, "National Merit Scholarship Qualifying Test," *The Fifth Measurements Yearbook,* Oscar K. Buros, ed. (Highland Park, New Jersey: The Gryphon Press, 1959), p. 21.

use of specific methods to produce Scholars became more frequent as one moved from rural to suburban and urban schools.

School personnel were not alone in their opinion that various methods are employed to increase the number of National Merit Scholars. Members of the press also contributed to the belief that special preparation is employed. In the concluding paragraph of an article pertaining to the "Merit Race" the following statement was made, "All (Semi-finalists) are expected to begin immediate cramming for the December examinations."[19]

Multiplicity of Testing

The National Merit Scholarship Program has become part of the multi-test approach to college admission and the awarding of scholarships. High school personnel, however, questioned the taking of so many standardized tests by the same students. Personnel who had been employed in the secondary schools for a period of twenty years or longer noted a loss of "local power of recommendation" and a reliance on test scores for scholarship and admission purposes.

Multiplicity of testing, of which the National Merit Scholarship Program was reported to be a part, appeared to be a cyclic phenomenon, one of preparing for tests, taking of tests, and using test results to prepare for still additional tests. In present day society, where an emphasis has been placed on examinations, perhaps it has become the task of the secondary school to guide graduating seniors through this maze of psychometrics.

Participation

Although there is no national policy stating that high schools *should* participate in the National Merit Scholarship Program, respondents were quite explicit in reporting that their schools were *expected* to participate in the National Merit Scholarship Program. Participation by the school, and in some cases, evidence of success in the program, seemed to satisfy community standards and a need for status. If the high schools were to withdraw from National Merit participation, school personnel felt that immediate questions would be asked by community members, whether they had been previously silent or vocal about the National Merit Scholarship Program.

National Merit participation and a high score on the National Merit Scholarship Qualifying Test have often resulted in the winning

---

[19]*Chicago Daily Tribune*, September 28, 1961, Pt. 4, 15.

50 Nationalizing Influences on Secondary Education

of other scholarships. The nationwide publicity given to high scorers on the Merit Test was thought to be of benefit to students attending high schools which have participated in the program. Inasmuch as the funds of the National Merit Scholarship Corporation are limited, the added advantage of a good performance on the National Merit Scholarship Qualifying Test leading to a subsequent scholarship offer from another source was recognized by many schools as reason enough for participating in the program. Thus, as shown in Table 4, participation continues to increase despite consistent lack of success, slim chances of obtaining a National Merit Scholarship, and disturbing community pressures. The National Merit Scholarship Qualifying Test results have also become a permanent part of the future college student's admission record.

TABLE 4

GROWTH OF THE
NATIONAL MERIT SCHOLARSHIP PROGRAM*

Year	No. of Contestants	Participating High Schools	No. of Finalists	Scholars	Participating Sponsors
1956	58,158	10,338	4,524	555	24
1957	166,592	12,502	7,255	827	58
1958	255,942	13,752	7,524	1,163	75
1959	478,991	14,454	9,868	920[a]	90
1960	550,221	14,549	10,181	1,008	115
1961	586,813	15,095	10,542	1,148	133

[a]Exhaustion of matching funds originally supplied by the Ford Foundation accounts for the drop in National Merit Scholarships.

*Sources: National Merit Scholarship Corporation, Annual Report 1961—Talent Our Prime National Resource (Evanston: National Merit Scholarship Corporation, 1962), pp. 30, 35; National Merit Scholarship Corporation, Annual Report, 1960 (Evanston: National Merit Scholarship Corporation, 1960), pp. 21, 30; National Merit Scholarship Corporation, Recognizing Exceptional Ability Among America's Young People, Fourth Annual Report, 1959 (Evanston: National Merit Scholarship Corporation, 1959), p. 3.

Guidance and Academic Incentive

One would assume that a test such as the National Merit Scholarship Qualifying Test, which includes English Usage, Mathematics Usage, Social Studies Reading, Natural Sciences Reading, and Word Usage, would be valued as a guidance tool. On the contrary, the guidance value of the National Merit Scholarship Qualifying Test, although reported as a form of National Merit impact, is of limited importance because of the variety and number of tests available for guidance purposes. The schools in the study reported that National Merit results are supplementary, serving as another index of a student's ability. In some cases National Merit results were reported as almost useless in the area of guidance because so many test results are available.

In agreement with Stalnaker's study,[20] the academic incentive of the program was reported as a form of National Merit impact. Statements ranged from, "the academic goals of the school coincide with the goals of the program," to "students want to be better scholars because of National Merit."

National Merit Policies

The selection of National Merit Scholars is made by a committee of evaluators, largely from the college admissions field. An advance press release issued by the Corporation stated:

> In addition to test scores, the selection committee considers the individuals' high school grades, accomplishments outside of the classroom, extra-curricular activities, school endorsements, and similar information submitted by the students and their schools. Special teams from many of the sponsoring organizations make selections from among those Finalists who met specific criteria, such as academic or career interest, geographical location, relationship to an employee of the sponsor, and the like. National Merit Scholarships and many of the sponsored scholarships are awarded without reference to preferential criteria of any kind, and each Finalist is evaluated for every such award.[21]

This selection process was questioned by respondents participating in the study. The most prevalent comment was, "The National Merit Scholarship Corporation does not select the student we (the high school personnel) think is the most deserving and best qualified to receive a scholarship." As mentioned previously, this process removes the selection of scholarship winners from the control of local school personnel.

With the announcement of an additional Ford Foundation grant

---

[20]Stalnaker reported, "In general, principals evaluated the National Merit Scholarship Program positively. In their opinion, the greatest single value of the program appeared to be the 'increased scholastic motivation' of the high-school students." See: John Stalnaker, "Principals Evaluate the National Merit Scholarship Program," *Bulletin of the National Association of Secondary School Principals*, XLII (March, 1958), 24.

[21]Press release prepared by William Young, Director of Public Relations, National Merit Scholarship Corporation, dated April 26, 1961, pp. 3-4.

52 Nationalizing Influences on Secondary Education

to the National Merit Scholarship Corporation, the editor of a daily newspaper stated:

> Part of the new grant will be used for research into better methods of identifying exceptionally bright boys and girls, . . . It isn't as easy to set up tests for brilliance, or special talents, or creativity as it was once thought, and some errors have crept into the selection process.[22]

The representation system, referred to by respondents as the "state quota system," has been used by the Corporation since the beginning of the Merit Program. The Corporation has stated:

> Since educational systems vary in different states, and are controlled by the separate states, it was deemed most equitable to allow students to participate in terms of competition with others in their states. This representation system, which corresponds to the methods used to apportion members of the House of Representatives is similar to that used in the selection of United States service academies' candidates, Rhodes Scholars, Markle Scholars, etc. It is used in the Merit Program and in similar undertakings because it permits the selection of a geographically diversified group of students representative of the best in the entire nation. Research data have indicated the soundness of this approach, for the very top-scoring students, regardless of state, consistently perform well in college.[23]

Respondents, in referring to the word national in the name of the Corporation, expressed the opinion that if it were truly a national program it would not consider state differences based on the number of graduating seniors in each state. It was thought that the representation practice was unfair to students in states where the required Qualifying Test score was extremely high. Respondents in a rural school located in a state assigned a high cut-off point objected to the unfair competition brought about by its geographic location. A newspaper article referred to the rural problem in the following manner:

> The competition for Merit Scholar ranking next spring is an internal one in each state.
>
> Scholarships are awarded in proportion to the number of seniors in each state. Thus rural Southern teen-agers are not competing with products of top city and suburban high schools in other sections of the country.[24]

Forgotten, however, are the rural teen-agers competing with products of top city and suburban schools in the same state.

---

[22]*Chicago Daily News*, April 7, 1962, 6.
[23]*Background Statement of the National Merit Scholarship Corporation*, (Evanston, Illinois: National Merit Scholarship Corporation, April 26, 1961), pp. 2-3.
[24]*Chicago Daily News*, September 27, 1961, p. 42.

Socio-economic Class

In testing the hypothesis that socio-economic class was related to level of success attained in the National Merit Scholarship Program, a correlation coefficient of .75 was derived, indicating that the ability to attain success in the National Merit Scholarship Program is related to the socio-economic background of the students. High schools enrolling students from upper and upper-middle class families attained higher levels of National Merit success than did high schools enrolling students from lower and lower-middle class families. Data from which this relationship may be inferred are shown in Table 5.

TABLE 5

NUMBER OF SCHOOLS REPORTING LEVEL OF SUCCESS IN THE NATIONAL MERIT SCHOLARSHIP PROGRAM BY SOCIO-ECONOMIC CLASS LEVEL OF COMMUNITY INHABITANTS

Level of Success in the NMSP	Lower-lower	Upper-lower	Lower-middle	Upper-middle	Upper
Scholar				5	1
Finalist		1	4	2	
Semi-finalist			2		
None*	1	2			
Total Number of Schools	1	3	6	7	1

*Not including Letter of Commendation level.

In summary, the impact of the National Merit Scholarship Program on the public high school has resulted in:

1. A rating of high schools on the basis of National Merit success (inclusive of a public use of the Program as a device for comparing schools).
2. The use of various methods of coaching designed to produce Scholars.
3. A recognition of the integral part played by the National Merit Scholarship Qualifying Test in the extensive multiple testing program which exists at the secondary school level.
4. A belief on the part of high school personnel that it is necessary to participate in this national program.

5. A general awareness of the importance of the program as a key to other scholarship opportunities and as an aid to college admission.
6. A recognition of the academic and guidance value of the National Merit Scholarship Program, although the latter form of impact was limited.
7. A discovery of respondent disagreement with some National Merit policies and procedures.

Conclusions

As noted above, the impact of the National Merit Scholarship Program on the public high school has assumed seven general forms; however, among these general forms, four are external to and removed from the direct control of the local high school. The forms of impact classified as external are: rating of high schools on the basis of National Merit results; "compulsory" participation in the National Merit Scholarship Program; "forced" membership in the multiple testing program; recognition of the importance of the program in relation to other scholarship opportunities and college admission.

The external rating of high schools has been one of the key factors affecting the internal impact of the program. Owing to the rating impact, administrators have made internal decisions to employ various coaching methods designed to produce Scholars and obtain public recognition. However, this decision depends on the type of community in which the school is located.

The guidance value of the program within the high school has been limited by one of the external forms of impact, the existence of a multiple testing program at the secondary school level. If the National Merit Scholarship Qualifying Test were the only test administered for scholarship and college admission purposes, its guidance value, undoubtedly, would increase. However, since the National Merit Scholarship Qualifying Test exists as a part of the multiple testing program, the test results sent to the schools by the Corporation have become part of a multitude of data available to counselors and high school students.

Participation in the National Merit Scholarship Program has also revealed that a program originating outside the immediate control of the secondary school has become an academic incentive in the eyes of secondary school students. Thus, although some forms of impact originate outside the school, they tend to influence the internal operation of the school.

As local educational institutions participate in national programs, the decision-making power of the local officials decreases. The National Merit Scholarship Program and other testing programs have removed from the hands of administrators the decision as to which tests should be used to determine college admission and scholarship winners. In a broader sense, the National Merit Scholarship Program has strengthened the practice which has been developing over a period of years, i.e., the awarding of scholarships on the basis of standardized test results rather than school records and local school recommendations. Participation in large scale testing programs has been undertaken by school administrators who view this large scale participation as the accepted and expected practice. In so doing, they have not fully realized that decisions have been made for them at the national level.

If the use of various methods designed to produce National Merit Scholars is indicative of administrative reaction to participation in national competitive programs, problems loom on the horizon. High school personnel protested as to the number of tests taken by secondary school students; nevertheless, additional tests were added to the schedule to prepare for the National Merit Scholarship Qualifying Test. Although staff members need to be cognizant of the power of the press and the importance of public relations, sound educational practices cannot be sacrificed for fleeting public acclaim. The National Merit Scholarship Program did not intend to provide the public with an educational measuring device, but the widespread publicity given to the program resulted in a comparison of schools. Knowing this, school personnel should not continue to blame the press or the Corporation for this rating, but should recognize that the pressures of the world situation have focused attention on the schools and demanded solutions to various types of problems.

The National Merit Scholarship Program which began as a search for talent has directed the attention of high school personnel to the college bound to the neglect of the terminal student. Guidance personnel and administrators have devoted more time to the college bound in an attempt to procure scholarships. Teachers, in some cases, have experienced pressure to produce scholarship winners. In some situations, where the level of academic achievement has not reached the required level in terms of scholarship awards, the morale of the student body has suffered.

On the other hand, participation in a national program has motivated staff members to strive for higher levels of achievement on the part of students. Students have discovered that failure to win an award in one program is not always indicative of future failure but may be a step toward winning an award in other programs.

This seems to indicate that local school participation in a national program has produced beneficial and harmful effects. The final classification of the forms of impact as beneficial or harmful depends on the background and values of the person so judging. However, it can be concluded that participation in the National Merit Scholarship Program has revealed that the public and the press are interested in and eager to rate schools if a convenient device is available. This rating, in turn, can be beneficial if it results in good public relations, improved curricular offerings, and motivation of faculty and student body. It can be harmful if it results in practices proved to be educationally unsound. It is also harmful if it leads to lower faculty and student body morale. School personnel concerned about the winning of scholarships have within their grasp the opportunity of providing students with a means of making college attendance possible. The decision as to the methods of preparation remains with school personnel. Consideration must be given to the amount of time which can and should be devoted to the college bound, and to the effect various methods of preparation will have on the students who are participating in the program and preparing for college attendance.

Finally, local school boards and administrators may have to give priority to certain external examinations as the multiple testing trend continues. The solution to the problem of increasing demands to use many tests will depend upon the forthright action of those charged with the operation of the schools in:

1. Determining the needs of their students and the time available for testing;
2. Choosing the testing programs meeting the above criteria; and
3. Educating their patrons in the need to support local decisions in the face of nationwide pressure to participate in every testing movement that comes along.

What will be required, then, will be educational leadership of a high order.

The National Defense Education Act of 1958

Arthur Kratzmann

Chapter 5

The National Defense Education Act was passed by the Senate on August 22, 1958 by a vote of 66 to 15 and a day later was approved in the House by a margin of 212 to 85. It was signed into Public Law 85-864 by President Eisenhower on September 2, 1958. The Act, a compromise between the original Hill-Elliott Bill and an Administration proposal, has a single stated purpose—"to provide substantial assistance in various forms to individuals, and to States and their subdivisions, in order to insure trained manpower of sufficient quality and quantity to meet the national defense needs of the United States." The Act, an aggregate of ten titles touching every level of public and private education from elementary through graduate school, was extended for a two-year period by the 87th Congress on September 26, 1961 and a week later was so signed into Public Law 87-400 by President Kennedy.

The purposes of this chapter are to: (a) examine briefly the antecedent forces leading to the enactment of the National Defense Education Act; (b) outline the provisions contained in the ten titles of the Act; (c) describe the increasing scope of the implementation of the legislation; (d) summarize some individual and group reactions to the Act; and (e) spell out what appear to be pertinent questions Americans might ask with respect to the National Defense Education Act and similar Federal enactments.

Antecedent Forces

The NDEA can be viewed as the first general effort to effect federal assistance to education at elementary and secondary levels. The aid given is categorical, but is much more diffuse in nature than in previous "educational" enactments. Although few perhaps share the enthusiasm of former Commissioner of Education Derthrick in stating that the Act is "a mighty complex," a "juncture of forces" moving us "surely onward toward our goal: Defense of our Nation against every enemy of body, mind, or spirit that time may bring,"[1] most would concede that the Act is a milestone in the development of educational policy at the national level.

Granting the importance of the Act, one is prompted to look for antecedents to such federal action. Basically, the aim of the Act is to improve certain facets of the educational system of the United States. But why was such improvement seen as being a task for federal action and support? And why did action, when taken, restrict itself to only a segment of the school's total sphere of operation? This chapter cannot analyze the many public and private, official and nonofficial antecedents to the Act, but will attempt to identify a number of significant forces which have been operative in the American society, particularly since World War II.

It is generally maintained that if the vitality of our democracy is to be preserved, our educational system must keep pace with an ever more complex society and the needs of a rapidly growing population. Consider the arguments offered by proponents of federal aid to education. Adequate schools with adequate staffs and adequate facilities for an increasing school population in a complex social setting can no longer be provided without help from the Federal Government.[2]

Thousands of school districts have exhausted their financial resources in attempting to keep pace with school needs. Going beyond the local level, the states have barely succeeded in maintaining the status quo in education, let alone take on that dynamism which is needed to keep abreast of a rapidly changing local, national, and international complex. Consequently, aid must come from sources beyond the states' boundaries. Furthermore, the qualitative differences in educational offerings arising from the imbalanced distribution of wealth in the nation deny many the opportunities for self-fulfillment and realization of potential that rightly belong to every person. The loss in human capital to the country is evident. Thus, these

---

[1] U. S. Department of Health, Education and Welfare, *Guide to the National Defense Education Act of 1958*, Circular 553, p. iv.

[2] See F. J. Seidner, *Federal Support for Education: The Situation Today* (Washington: The Public Affairs Institute, 1959), pp. i-ii.

shortcomings observed by proponents of federal aid could only be remedied by a new and higher level of shared responsibility and cooperation, involving federal action and support.

The recent surging growth and development of this nation as a world power and the awareness of responsibilities which are attendant with such international status have obviously given added impetus to federal action in support of education. Professional educators and insightful laymen have looked with concern at the shortages, in both quantity and quality, of the teaching force; at the fact that the degree of foreign language instruction in the United States over the past forty years has been inversely related to the country's rise as a world power;[3] at the statistics indicating that about 100,000 able high school students each year fail to go to college because of some lack of guidance and motivation; and at the alarming shortages of well-trained scientists and technicians in a highly automated world. The campaigns of the many persons who vocalized their anxieties on the above and related issues could well have provided most of the language for the titles of the National Defense Education Act.[4]

When the problems outlined above are examined in a setting of national responsibilities for the preservation of the democratic way of life in the free world, and at the same time a discerning eye is turned to the methods and achievements of those who would undermine such efforts internationally, concern and anxiety for many has turned to fervor and panic. When Dr. Edward Teller testified before the Senate Preparedness Investigating Subcommittee that "young people in Russia . . . have a considerably better science education than similar age groups in this country . . . (and) it is a foregone conclusion that they will do a better job,"[5] he was voicing the concern of the whole nation with respect to Soviet advances in the technical world.

The immediate catalyst which hastened what many had considered to be the unavoidable modification of ways and means of

---

[3] Gerald W. Elbers, "NDEA and Higher Education," *Higher Education* XVI (September, 1959), 9.
[4] For discussion of the relationship of antecedent forces to legal enactments, see Roald F. Campbell, "Antecedents and Expressions of Educational Policy at the National Level," *Education Research Bulletin*, XXXVIII (September, 1959), 141-50.
[5] Seidner, *loc. cit.*

supporting and guiding education in the United States was Sputnik. And while there were and are many who would support Congressman Frank Thompson of New Jersey in his stand that the defense aspect of the Act was a "gimmick" to get it through the Congress at a time when national emotions were riding high, the House member reaction and vote would tend to reveal that most agreed with Alabama Congressman Carl Elliott, chairman of the Special Education Subcommittee, who stated that "There is a real good reason for each title in the bill . . . each has its place . . . and will serve a very worthy purpose in doing what we want to do for America, namely, to answer the Soviet threat to gain supremacy over us in science."[6]

Provisions and Implementation of the Act

During its first four years of operation, the National Defense Education Act authorized over one billion dollars in aid. The Act is administered under ten titles. The first of these sets forth the general purposes of the Act as well as a definition of terms; the others outline, and authorize funds for, the various programs of aid. Except for Title IX, which establishes a special service in the National Science Foundation, the Act is administered at the federal level by the United States Office of Education.

As shown in Table 6, approximately 60 per cent of the appropriated funds have been distributed as grants to State educational agencies for strengthening instruction in the elementary and secondary schools (Title III), testing and counseling (Title V), providing area vocational education (Title VIII), and improving statistical services (Title X). The remainder has gone to institutions of higher learning for loans to students (Title II), fellowships (Title IV), institutes to train counselors (Title V), and foreign language centers and institutes (Title VI); and to agencies, organizations, and individuals for research in educational utilization of television, radio, motion pictures, and related media of communication (Title VII).

Before the funds have been put into the hands of the recipients, a number of prerequisites have been met, for the Office of Education and for the States and Institutions of higher education. The Office

---

[6]For a discussion of this controversy, see Elaine Exton, "Administration of Defense Education Law Still Controversial," *American School Board Journal*, CXXXVIII (June, 1959), 46-47.

has had to draw up regulations to take care of the multitude of administrative details not specified in the Act but necessary to assure consistency and impartiality of allocation of funds. Some states have had to receive authorization from their legislatures to receive federal aid before they could initiate programs for the use of such assistance. Conditions are further complicated by the fact that States must match federal funds dollar for dollar (although this was not necessary in the first year for some programs). Moreover, any State or institution of education must submit to the U. S. Commissioner of Education its plan for using federal monies. Although such plans have to be comprehensive and long-range in nature, they are not irrevocably binding and may be revised as circumstances change. More specific provisions of the Act are to be found in publications of the U. S. Office of Education.

> By June, 1959, every State and Territory (with the exception of the Panama Canal Zone, which is not participating for reasons of a local nature) had filed and had received approval of at least one State plan, and more than four out of five had had as many as three plans.[7]

This degree of involvement is significant in that the first year was one of resolving administrative difficulties and of taking minor legislative action to assure smoother operation of the Act. By the end of the following year (fiscal 1960) all programs were clearly "in full swing." While this chapter will not attempt to detail all the programs which have been developed, several examples will serve to highlight the impact which the NDEA made during its first two years.

By 1960, some 1,357 of the 1,950 institutions of higher education in this country were participating under Title II in the student loan program, and 115,450 students had received financial aid. It is interesting to note that 639 of the participating colleges and universities had never had loan funds on their campuses before, and that many others were modifying their existing loan funds in the light of NDEA practices. The U.S. Office of Education claims that the loan program "has all but reversed earlier student and parental attitudes toward borrowing to finance a college education."[8]

Enrollments in science, mathematics, and modern foreign language courses in secondary schools increased more rapidly than did total school enrollments during the first two years of the administra-

---

[7] U. S., Dept. of Health, Education, and Welfare, *Report on the National Defense Education Act,* June 30, 1959, Circular OE-10004, 2.
[8] *Ibid.,* pp. 5-6.

TABLE 6
NDEA AUTHORIZATIONS AND APPROPRIATIONS FOR FISCAL YEARS 1959 THROUGH 1962*
(IN MILLIONS OF DOLLARS)

Title	1959 Authorization	1959 Appropriation	1959 % of Total Appropriation	1960 Authorization	1960 Appropriation	1960 % of Total Appropriation
II. Loans to Students in Institutions of Higher Learning	47.50	31.00	27.6	75.00	40.70	25.6
III. Financial Assistance for Science, Mathematics, and Modern Foreign Language Instruction	75.00	57.35	49.3	75.00	64.00	40.1
IV. National Defense Graduate Fellowships	(1)	5.30	4.5	(1)	12.65	7.9
V. Guidance, Counseling and Testing	21.25	10.80	9.3	22.25	20.50	12.7
VI. Language Development	15.25	5.00	4.3	15.25	10.60	6.6
VII. Media Research and Experimentation	3.00	1.60	1.4	5.00	3.10	1.9
VIII. Area Vocational Education Programs	15.00	3.75	3.2	15.00	7.00	4.4
X. Improvement of Statistical Services of State Educational Agencies	2.75	.49	.4	2.75	1.13	.8
TOTALS		$115.29			$159.68	

TABLE 6 (Continued)

Title	1961 Authorization	1961 Appropriation	1961 % of Total Appropriation	1962 Authorization	1962 Appropriation	1962 % of Total Appropriation
II. Loans to Students in Institutions of Higher Learning	82.50	58.46	31.2	90.00	75.15	35.5
III. Financial Assistance for Science, Mathematics, and Modern Foreign Language Instruction	75.00	57.75	30.8	75.00	57.75	27.4
IV. National Defense Graduate Fellowships	(1)	20.70	11.0	(1)	22.26	10.5
V. Guidance, Counseling and Testing	22.25	21.50	11.5	22.25	22.10	10.3
VI. Language Development	7.25 and (1)	13.80	7.4	7.25 and (1)	15.25	7.2
VII. Media Research and Experimentation	5.00	4.73	2.5	5.00	4.77	2.3
VIII. Area Vocational Education Programs	15.00	9.00	4.8	15.00	12.80	6.0
X. Improvement of Statistical Services of State Educational Agencies	(1)	1.50	.8	(1)	1.55	.7
TOTALS		$187.44			$211.63	

(1) As necessary
*Sources: NDEA Annual Reports for 1959, 1960 and Financial Assistance Programs, 1962 Edition, published by the U. S. Office of Education.

tion of Title III. Some states have experienced as much as a 50 per cent increase in mathematics and science classes; the national percentage increase in enrollments in modern foreign language courses from the fall of 1958 to the fall of 1959 was greater than for the preceding four years combined. The year 1959 saw 31 states participating in 8,947 projects; by the following year, 51 states and territories were involved in 47,976 such projects. The number of language laboratories in the nation mushroomed from 64 in 1958 to 1,000 in June of 1960. There was a marked trend toward the purchasing of large amounts of equipment and materials for mathematics and science instruction for elementary schools where, before the Act, these tools of learning were almost nonexistent. State educational agencies have greatly increased their leadership staff in the above subject areas, showing a five-fold increase in science, mathematics, and modern foreign language supervisors during the two-year period under examination. The consequent influence of these supervisors has been seen in the publication of 118 new curriculum guides in their subject fields.

Title V received a doubled appropriation from 1959 to 1960. During the period of operation of the Act, there has been a change in the nation's counselor-student ratio from 1:750 in 1958 to 1:610 in 1960. During 1959, under the same title, a total of 2,117,526 ability and aptitude tests were administered in public and non-public secondary schools for guidance purposes; by 1960 the number of such tests had risen to 19,562,000. During the two years, 203 counseling and guidance training institutes were conducted in 47 states, the District of Columbia, and Puerto Rico. The number of State supervisors in guidance rose from 99 to 255.

Reinforced by a year of experience and supported by an increased appropriation, language institutes were tripled in number from 1959 to 1960. In all, 2,943 teachers participated during the two-year period in programs of French, German, Spanish, Russian, and Italian languages.

Other activities under the remaining titles of the Act included benefits to 2,500 graduate students who received NDEA fellowships in 155 institutions of learning; 120 projects for research and experimentation in more effective use of audio-visual materials in education were approved in 34 states; 48 states, the District of Columbia, and Puerto Rico amended their established plans for area vocational education programs; and 40 states evaluated the existing statistical services of their educational agencies and added personnel in an attempt to provide more effective services.

Statistically, the record that has been established in carrying out the provisions of the National Defense Education Act is a formidable one. There has been a sharp acceleration of activity under every title, and one can hardly deny that federal assistance is bringing new resources continually to the American educational system. It is anticipated that this momentum will be sustained.

Reactions to the Act

Reports emanating from the United States Office of Education are understandably tinged through emotional involvement when describing the many successful facets of the National Defense Education Act. Consequently they fail to give a complete portrayal of the general reaction to the legislation. In order to secure a wider cross-section of responses, nearly all periodical literature bearing upon the Act since its inception in 1958 was surveyed. Again, these reactions are rife with limitations. In the first place, really penetrating articles are very few in number; secondly, they are almost completely the responses of professional educators; and finally, most of the views need to be filtered through objective lenses since they are charged with emotionality and are "heavy on hunches."

Global Responses

In general, it would appear that professional educators who have a direct operational interest in the provisions of the legislation are favorably disposed to the Act, although there is indeed no degree of unanimity in the professional ranks. Business and agricultural organizations, on the other hand, are opposed to federal aid by and large and especially to categorical aid, and consequently doubt its effectiveness and question the justification for the continued operation of the Act. The National Association of Manufacturers and the Chamber of Commerce of the United States are among such groups. A third general response comes from special interest groups, including the National Catholic Education Association, the Association for Childhood Education, and the National Association for Gifted Children, who call for an extension of the Act to promote areas of education with which they are directly concerned.

More specific arguments are associated with (a) a general evaluation of the effect of the Act upon the improvement of education; (b) the question of federal aid *per se*, as well as the nature of such aid; (c) the bureaucratic administrative features of the Act; (d) the possible curriculum imbalances created by the legislation; (e) the budgeting procedures of local school districts; and (f) inequitable aid distributions. Each of these issues will be discussed in turn.

Evaluation of the Act in Terms of Improvement of Education

The U.S. Office of Education literature is alive with anecdotal responses of persons and groups in school systems who have benefited from NDEA participation. In their totality, these responses take on significance. There is every indication that a great number of school districts have explicitly reappraised their present school programs, have raised equipment standards, have striven to employ more qualified personnel, have sought out more effective instructional materials, and have articulated more carefully their programs of instruction at all levels. To what degree any of these things would have occurred without formal enactment of the NDEA can never be known. Many schoolmen claim that improvements they have undertaken within the framework of the Act were already slated for action in their districts; others claim that NDEA merely hastened their actions by a year or two. The only thing to note is that these things have been done and, without applying any causal logic, to recognize that one cannot escape the realities of the relationship between legislation and educational advances. To determine the magnitude of these advances would be a most complex task. Walker has suggested that:

> To assess the effect upon the improvement of education as a consequence of the National Defense Education Act at this early date would be sheer folly. At best, one can tabulate the changes effected through the implementation of the legislation. We can then assume that, with added services, new and better teaching tools, better trained teachers, and increased emphasis, we are better accepting the Congress implied responsibility for the security of the nation through improved education.[9]

Federal Aid

Reactions to the type of aid, as well as to the matter of aid itself from federal sources as provided by the NDEA merely reopens an old controversy. The antagonists form into three groups—those who oppose federal assistance of any kind in the educational realm, the few who appear to favor such assistance in any shape or form, and the seeming majority who prefer general as against categorical aid. Those in the second group above feel encouraged to have broken through the hard crust of resistance to federal aid and at long last to

---

[9] Otto V. Walker, Proceedings of the 45th Annual Convention, *Bulletin of the National Association of Secondary-School Principals*, XLIV (April, 1961), 139.

have established a beach-head in the federal forum.[10] Business and agricultural organizations are generally opposed to federal aid in any shape or form, their opposition stemming from the near-legendary "threat of Federal control" and the "fear of encroachment on State and local educational prerogatives." The majority of organizations believe that future federal assistance should not follow the pattern of categorical aid provided by the NDEA.[11] The Executive Committee of the AASA believes that the "Congress should pass a general support bill for the operation and capital improvement of public schools, with the specific use being determined by states and local school authorities."[12] The Council of Chief State School Officers has endorsed this position and urged that allocations of Federal funds should constitute an additional revenue source which the states can apply to the most critical areas of educational expenditure.[13]

However, many educators who are very familiar with the operation of the Act maintain that to discuss spreading aid to fields other than those specified in the legislation itself is purely academic, since in actual practice NDEA funds which are returned to the states under the reimbursement schedules in state plans have indirectly aided curriculum areas other than those encompassed by the Act.[14]

Bureaucratic Features of Administration

Mention has already been made of the administrative machinery which has been instituted to assure smooth and impartial operation of the Act. And while one cannot question the need for administrative structure, many persons, and particularly Chief State School Officers, have been overwhelmed by the mass of specifications, regulations, and details associated with the preparation and approval of state plans. In some instances, anxiety over the bureaucratic mechanics appears to have spilled over and generated a more deep-seated concern for the whole Federal-State relationship, for nowhere is control more

---

[10]J. C. Whinnery, "Toehold, Now for a Foothold," *Phi Delta Kappan*, XL (October, 1958), 36.

[11]The reactions of a large number of professional and nonprofessional groups are discussed in Sidney C. Sufrin, "Administering the NDEA," Research in Educational France Project of the Maxwell Graduate School of Citizenship and Public Affairs (Syracuse University, 1962).

[12]Arthur H. Rice, "NDEA Is an Unwise Compromise," *Nation's Schools*, LXVII (February, 1961), 61.

[13]*Ibid.*

[14]For a discussion of this practice, see Elaine Exton, "Problems in Administration of the NDEA," *American School Board Journal*, CXLII (March, 1961), 40.

sharply evidenced than in the written prerequisites for aid. The question of "Why all the detail," then becomes, "Are we not tending to establish a federal control which was the very thing all of us, including Congress, hoped to avoid?"[15] And while one cannot argue convincingly that administrative minutiae and administrative control are clearly intertwined, requirements such as the submission of thirty copies of a single research proposal, for example, do little to unravel the knot in the perceptions of participants.

Curriculum Imbalances

The U.S. Office of education claims that:

> Although designed to strengthen American education at selected, strategic points of critical National need, the National Defense Education Act has generated a tremendous upward surge that is benefiting every phase and every element of American education.[16]

There is some evidence that school systems are evaluating total programs in drawing up long-range objectives in terms of NDEA participation, but there are those who are convinced that imbalances are being created. Many special interest groups, and particularly educators in fields other than guidance, mathematics, science, and modern foreign languages believe that the Act has discriminated against many curriculum areas. According to this view, the need exists for improved facilities and teaching materials in all subjects, and especially for equitable training opportunities for all teachers.

In reacting to this last point, Rice maintains that, without in any way diminishing the efforts of public education to provide the scientists, linguists, and technicians needed, any emergency program should emphasize all the major purposes of public education in a democratic society such as ours.[17]

Local School District Budgeting

There are conflicting responses with regard to local district fiscal attitudes and actions. Some critics adamantly claim that the National Defense Education Act has gradually become a "boon-doggle" in which many school districts are spending beyond their means and needs in order to get federal returns and feel that educators react to federal money in a fashion similar to all pressure groups when con-

---

[15] Exton, *American School Board Journal*, CXXXVIII (June, 1959), 46.

[16] U. S. Dept. of Health, Education, and Welfare, *Report on the National Defense Education Act, June 30, 1960*, Circular OE-10004-60, 2.

[17] Rice, *Nation's Schools*, LXVII (February, 1961), 61.

fronted by a windfall.[18] Campbell and Hencley found, however, a striking number of city school systems in their survey who were not dependent on NDEA aid or who had not requested allocations under the Act.[19] Then again, there remains the fact that Federal funds in many instances have been over-matched. This is particularly true under Title III where many states have gone beyond NDEA minimum equipment standards. It would seem unwise to attribute the degree or nature of local spending or the absence of it to the influences of federal legislation.

Inequitable Aid Distributions

Many school administrators claim that the National Defense Education Act places its support behind larger and more prosperous school districts. On a matching basis, it is felt that the smaller and less financially able areas are unable to complete in terms of a per capita expenditure for each student in the areas of instruction being supported. The single purpose outlined in the initial administrative guide to the Act that "every young person, from the day he first enters school, should have the opportunity to develop his gifts to the fullest"[20] seems to infer a philosophy of equalization which appears to be in jeopardy in the world of reality.

Some Pertinent Questions

The foregoing sections of this chapter suggest a number of long-range questions which need to be answered. Most of these have already been proposed by Campbell,[21] but along with others, they are worthy of repetition since answers have not been readily forthcoming.

1. Are national educational emergencies stable? Section 101 of the Act declares that: "The present emergency demands that additional and more adequate educational opportunities be made available." The Act was a response to the emergency as perceived in 1958 and apparently again in 1961 when the Act was extended. But will the nature of the emergency have remained unchanged for six years?

---

[18]*Ibid.*, p. 86.

[19]Roald F. Campbell and Stephen P. Hencley, "Accept NDEA Money, but with Doubts and Reservations," *Nation's Schools*, LXVI (October, 1960), 80-83.

[20]U. S., Dept. of Health, Education, and Welfare, *Guide to the National Defense Education Act of 1958*, 1.

[21]Roald F. Campbell, "The Impact of the National Defense Education Act on Public Schools," *Administrator's Notebook*, VIII (January, 1960).

Does the emergency still, in fact, exist? What evaluation, if any, is being pursued to gauge national needs in education?

2. Has federal control of education been "prohibited"? Section 102 declares: "Nothing contained in this Act shall be construed to authorize any department, agency, officer, or employee of the United States to exercise any direction, supervision, or control over the curriculum, program of instruction, administration, or personnel of any educational institution or school systems." What is meant here by direction and control? If one accepts the Webster meaning of control as the "authority to direct or regulate" and applies it to the categorical nature of NDEA aid and to the submission of proposals which are often not approved until regulatory requirements are met, then Section 102 tends to become a collection of verbal symbols without significance.

3. How much "local control" really exists in education today? The Act declares that "the States and local communities have and must retain control over and primary responsibility for public education." And this stand is substantiated by those individuals and groups who oppose NDEA because it threatens to take away local control. It is not that either local or federal control is necessarily a good or a bad thing. But until it is decided what control is, and who has and does possess it in the educational realm, further discussions of the subject cannot be rationally based.

4. What does the NDEA mean in terms of future federal legislative patterns for education? State Departments are becoming increasingly involved in the administration and supervision of funds and services provided by the NDEA. Is it not reasonable to assume that, as they have come not only to depend upon such aid but to sanction it as well, they will be tempted to call for assistance in areas not already covered by the present ten titles? The Act forms a structure that could be extended readily through legislative approval. Can one then look for an extension along lines of further categorical aid? And if enough categories are eventually added, would the situation not be coming close to the general federal support so widely advocated? Pertinent to these questions is a comment by Rice, who perhaps senses that there are inconsistencies in the stand of those who want aid given to other areas in education, but who at the same time are concerned with the preservation of appropriate Federal-State relationships. He asks, "If, under the present Act, Congress exerts strong influence over

30 to 40 per cent of the curriculum, does it remedy the situation to extend Congressional control to 60 to 80 per cent of the curriculum?"[22]

5. Have American national needs superseded the long established rights of individuals? Campbell poses this question most succinctly:

> The essence of the democratic credo has been the enhancement of the individual. The state has been seen as the servant of the individual and not the reverse. Basic to this position is the assumption that free individuals will take the steps necessary to insure group welfare. "Education for defense," on the other hand, places the emphasis on the social need, not on individual development. Able students are to be identified as a national resource. Many of them are to be given financial aid to help them become scientist soldiers for national survival. Is it possible that in order to meet the threat of our chief antagonist we have adopted the very values which we wish to resist?[23]

Summary

This chapter has examined briefly the antecedent forces operative in the American and world societies which bear a relationship to the enactment of the National Education Defense Act of 1958. Chief among these appear to have been the need for new ways and means of financing American public education, a concern for apparent weaknesses in American education, and a growing sense of national responsibility for the free and democratic world. The provisions of the Act were next described and attention was drawn to the accelerating impact of the legislation during the two-year period discussed in this chapter.

The major portion of the chapter has been devoted to the reactions of groups and individuals to the 1958 legislation. These may be summarized as follows:

1. Globally, educators appear to be favorably disposed to the Act; business and agricultural organizations, stand opposed to Federal control, doubt the effectiveness of the legislation and question its continued operation; special interest groups call for extensions of the Act to promote areas of direct concern to them.

2. There is considerable evidence that the implementation of the Act bears a relationship to the appraisal and upgrading of instructional personnel, facilities, and offerings of many American school districts. There is no consensus of opinion as to the actual cause and effect relationships which may exist.

3. The "Federal aid" controversy has been reopened as a result

---

[22]Rice, *op. cit.*, p. 62.
[23]Campbell, *op. cit.*

of the NDEA. Many individuals and organizations would appear to favor general as against categorical Federal assistance for education.

4. There are some concerns felt regarding the bureaucratic nature of the implementation of the Act by federal officials. This is particularly true in the case of chief state school officers who are overwhelmed by the administrative minutiae connected with the implementation of the Act.

5. Many educators are convinced that curriculum imbalances have been created by the Act. Special interest groups are particularly vocal in this regard.

6. Many school administrators claim that the NDEA has placed its support behind the larger and more financially able school districts, with which the poorer and smaller districts cannot compete. The inferred philosophy of equalization in the Act would thus appear to be in jeopardy.

Finally, growing out of the above considerations, a number of long-range issues have been raised. These are related to: the assessment of the nature of the emergency which preceded passage of the Act; the nature and degree of control over public education exercised by the three levels of government; the Act as an indicator of future federal legislative patterns pertaining to public education; and, to the relationship of the NDEA to the democratic credo.

This chapter is limited by the subjective elements found in both the documents prepared by the U.S. Office of Education and the majority of the writings in periodical literature which focus on the Act. The purpose of this chapter has been realized if the reader is challenged to look again at the NDEA, and to seriously consider its value and impact in his school district, and its implications for American education.

The College Entrance Examination Board

Lester Przewlocki

Chapter 6

Background

From a rather modest beginning some sixty years ago on the campus of Columbia University, the College Entrance Examination Board has risen to a place of prominence and influence in American secondary education. If the past in any way portends the future, one might suspect that this prominence and influence will continue to increase. Moreover, the influence of the College Entrance Examination Board is not confined to this country alone—its work is prevalent in more than seventy foreign countries as well.

That the College Board is regarded as an influential force by secondary schools can be seen in chapters two, seven, and eight. Hence, this chapter will not attempt to document that point, but rather will narrate, somewhat briefly, the history of the development of the various programs and activities of the College Board. It has long been accepted that the College Board is the leader in the field of college admissions testing, and consequently, the literature in the field during the past decade is relatively devoid of defenses or attacks on the basic testing programs such as the Scholastic Aptitude or Preliminary Scholastic Aptitude Tests. Rather, the emphasis, and presumably, the interest today lies in the Advanced Placement Programs sponsored by the College Board. More space will be given to this latter program because it seems to represent a signal achievement in American education.

The main purpose of the College Board has changed little since Nicholas Murray Butler, first secretary of the Board, and later to become an outstanding president of Columbia University, gave his first report in 1901:

74 Nationalizing Influences on Secondary Education

It is quite untrue that the aim of the college admission examination is, primarily, to test the work of the secondary schools. That is merely incidental to its main purpose, which is to ascertain whether a pupil is well enough equipped for more advanced study in college or a scientific school.

. . . The work of the Board will promptly elevate the secondary school work in English, in history, and in the natural sciences to a new plane of importance and of effectiveness. It will control the examination system in the interest of education and resist the tendency to make it a mere machine-like performance. It will declare and enforce standards of attainment which represent, not the labors of a zealous individual, however wise, but the mature judgment of a group of mature scholars of different training and points of view.[1]

The representatives of eleven eastern universities and of six secondary schools who formed the College Entrance Examination Board of the Middle States and Maryland, later to be known simply as the College Entrance Examination Board, agreed that the work of the Board was to construct and administer examinations to secondary school students applying for admission to college. They further agreed that they would accept the results of the examination as a satisfactory substitute for their own entrance examinations, since, they reasoned, the topics covered in the Board's examination were virtually the same as their own.

The idea of an independent agency administering and conducting entrance examinations caught on rather slowly, although in its first year (1901) almost 1000 candidates took the examination offered by the Board. By 1910 almost 4000 candidates applied for the examination in what was destined to become an ever growing and far reaching testing program. By 1960 nearly 750,000 secondary students participated in the College Board examinations. Further, 427 colleges and universities, 126 secondary schools, and 42 educational associations were listed as members of the Board in that same year. These figures do not include the many nonmember schools who may and do use the facilities and the services of this organization.

Because of its increasing and expanding role and because its patrons were demanding more service, and because of the sheer numbers of applicants who were seeking college admission, the College Board, in 1959, established regional offices in the Midwest, the South, and the Far West. In 1961, it also established a Northeast regional office in New York.

---

[1]College Entrance Examination Board of the Middle States and Maryland, *First Annual Report of the Secretary* (New York: College Entrance Examination Board, 1901), p. 30 ff.

The business of the CEEB is conducted at an annual meeting of its membership and by action of an elected Board of Trustees. The supervision of all major programs of the Board is by special and standing committees appointed by the chairman of the Board. There are committees on Examinations, Membership, Research and Development, Entrance Procedures, Guidance, Advanced Placement, and College Scholarship Services.

Membership in the College Board is relatively simple to obtain; any college or university that is accredited by the proper regional accrediting agency and which makes substantial use of at least one of the Board's regular admission tests may apply. As of the October 25, 1962 meeting of the Board, there were 427 colleges and universities who were members, 76 of which were admitted to membership at that time. Annual membership dues for the colleges are fifty dollars and for educational associations and secondary schools the dues are twenty five dollars. Although nonmember schools and colleges may use the tests offered by the Board, they are not entitled to membership privileges nor are they entitled to send official representatives to the meetings of the Board.

Secondary schools, prior to 1959, had only an indirect voice in the affairs of the CEEB, and this through the various educational associations to which they belonged or through service of school personnel as elected officers or committee members. Recognizing, however, that secondary schools were concerned with the many questions and problems of admission and advanced standing, the Board has elected secondary schools to become full members of the CEEB since 1959. At present, 165 high schools are members, 39 of which were elected in 1962. These elected schools serve three year terms on a rotating basis in order to give as many schools as possible the opportunity to participate in the policy-making function of the Board. Representation is established according to the type of school, its regional location, its size, and the number of candidates who take the tests and examinations of the CEEB.

Entrance Testing

Most high school seniors are familiar with the *Scholastic Aptitude Test* (SAT) which is designed to provide some reliable indications of a student's ability to do college work. This three hour-long objective test is scored on a scale which ranges from a low of 200 to a high of 800. The Board does not attempt to evaluate the results of the SAT but forwards the scores to the college indicated by the candidate for evaluation and interpretation. Because the scale of the tests is the same for all editions whenever and wherever it is administered, it presumably provides admission counselors with a standardized instrument which purports to measure the same kinds of ability in all parts of the country.

Martin Mayer[2] in examining the whole question of tests and examinations comments that the Scholastic Aptitude Tests measure little more than reading ability and social class difference. Somewhat critically, he further comments that while many colleges use the results of the SAT as one major criterion for college admission—

> Prestige colleges accept from well-known private preparatory schools without much reference to the individual boy's Scholastic Aptitude scores, because they trust the observation and the judgment of the schools' headmasters. In the real world, real judgments are made on the observation of colleagues or employers, who have watched a man at work, not on the results of paper-and-pencil tests.[3]

Even if this observation is true it is quite apparent that more and more emphasis is being placed on the SAT and its effect filters into other areas as well. For example, one "Big Ten" athletic director puts it this way:

> Almost every college football player receives a grant-in-aid, but in order to qualify for such financial help the player must take an entrance exam, either the Scholastic Aptitude Test or the Accredited College Test, and have a projected grade expectancy of 2.75, which is a C minus.
>
> Any youngster who passes these tests is fairly certain to be able to remain scholastically eligible.[4]

Although the College Board reiterates frequently that its tests are not susceptible to coaching, there are many publications on the market which profess to replicate the College Board tests and amply prepare the prospective candidate for the admission examinations. There are some, however, who recognize that the high selectivity procedures of the colleges promote coaching apparently with the sanction and the blessing of the schools.

> Testing enthusiasts with ambitious promoters have been quick to cash in on the insecurity of both educators and parents by publishing booklets that promise to prepare students for that fatal day—

---

[2]Martin Mayer, *The Schools* (New York: Harper and Brothers, 1961), p. 373.
[3]*Ibid.*, p. 377.
[4]*Chicago Sun Times,* October 31, 1962, 64.

the day when the entrance exam will descend upon them like the very sword of Damocles. . . .

Year by year, we go on proliferating the traffic in external testing by our very support of such practices. We continue to support publishers in their efforts to foist upon our unsuspecting students a whole series of tests, purported to train them to do better on the College Board examinations.[5]

The College Board reaches farther down into the secondary school when it offers and administers the *Preliminary Scholastic Aptitude Test* (PSAT) to third year students. Similar in design to the SAT, this test is given for the early guidance of high school juniors. In 1959, the first year this test was given, over 600,000 students participated; in 1961, more than 700,000 juniors took these preliminary tests. Although the program is attracting more students, and although it would seem that the secondary schools are embracing the program with the same enthusiasm as the SAT, a California superintendent of schools questions the practice and the apparent contradiction in the College Board's statements:

> Even Educational Testing Service has succumbed to our test-happy demands by scheduling the 'preliminary scholastic aptitude test' for juniors so that the shock of taking the scholastic aptitude test in their senior year will be softened—all this, despite the statements of college admissions boards that no amount of practice in taking these tests will serve to improve the final result.[6]

Another kind of testing program which has gained popularity in recent years is the subject matter achievement testing which is offered to high school seniors after the administration of the Scholastic Aptitude Tests. There are achievement tests in the following subjects: Intermediate and Advanced Mathematics, French, German, Spanish, Greek, Italian, Latin, Hebrew, Russian, Social Studies, Biology, Chemistry, Physics, and English Composition. For the most part, these tests are of the objective type, are one hour long, and are scored similarly to the SAT on a scale from 200 to 800.

As in the case of the SAT, the tests are scored by the Board but not evaluated. This again is left to the college admissions officers of the university chosen by the candidate. High school counselors also receive the scores, and may, if they so desire, reveal the scores to the student.

The strength of the testing program and the interest it has gen-

---

[5]Ernest G. Lake, "The Case Against External Standardized Tests," *The Nation's Schools*, LXX (August, 1962), 52-53.

[6]*Ibid.*, p. 53.

erated is demonstrated by the fact that the achievement tests are offered at more than 1700 centers throughout the United States and 70 foreign countries. As the emphasis on college training increases, as the secondary school population increases, and as the number of seats available in the universities decreases, undoubtedly, the number of students and the number of institutions participating in the Achievement Testing Program will increase.

All of the aforementioned testing programs are conducted by Educational Testing Service, an independent, nonprofit agency founded in 1948 with the support of the CEEB, the Carnegie Foundation, and the American Council on Education. It also conducts a major portion of the College Board's large research program and administers testing programs for other educational organizations.

College Scholarship Service

Another service of the College Board frequently used by the colleges is the College Scholarship Service. It was established in 1954 to assist college-bound candidates who feel the need for financial help, and to communicate both this fact and the degree of need to as many colleges as the student may choose. With more than 400 participating colleges forming this association, the Service provides a forum for the exchange of ideas on financial aid problems and policies, and in addition, conducts research on aid matters.

Advanced Placement Programs

For the past decade there has been increasing activity by colleges, universities, and secondary schools to provide challenging programs for the academically superior student. Honors courses, credit by examination, independent study programs, and advanced standing are being examined somewhat more critically by college faculties.

For many years one method of providing a greater intellectual challenge for the superior student has been to allow him to accelerate one or more grades, although this practice is more frequent in the elementary school than in the secondary school. Occasionally, at the college level, students were accepted who had not completed a basic high school course but who were academically superior. In 1951, the Program of Early Admission to College, started by a group of twelve colleges and universities, provided extensive and carefully analyzed tests of the effect of admitting students to college who had only completed the second or third year of high school, and who, on the average, were one or two years younger than other freshmen.

The Fund for the Advancement of Education gave financial support to this program which had 1350 students participating. These students throughout their college years were carefully compared with selected control groups of students who were in all respects alike except that they had not entered college earlier and were somewhat older.

The experimental program provided some good evidence that the early-admission students would not be injured academically or socially. Paschal[7] states that the "evidence was overwhelmingly favorable toward this approach to the problem of freeing the able student from the academic lockstep and permitting him to move forward at a pace suited to his capabilities."

Recognizing that administrators and teachers were reluctant to see their most able students lost to them during the last two years of high school, and further recognizing that the practice of early admission to college might impose some financial problems on the family, in that college admission would occur two years earlier than anticipated, another group formed the School and College Study of Admission with Advanced Standing. This group believed a student should remain with his class but do college level work in one or more courses, which would enable him, when the courses were completed, to enter college with advanced standing. Seven schools served as pioneers in the experiment of giving their students—their able students—special courses prepared by a study group and of testing their competence by examinations set by an outside group.

In 1954 the work of this group culminated in a report which presented course outlines, examinations, and the administration of eleven freshmen courses. Those colleges which had participated in the initial program agreed that students who had completed the described work, and passed the examinations were well qualified for placement at an advanced level.

Since 1955 the College Entrance Examination Board has sponsored and conducted the Advanced Placement Program which provides the superior high school student the opportunity to receive appropriate placement, credit, or both on the basis of college level courses which have been taken in high school. The Program is based on the premise

---

[7]Elizabeth Paschal, *Encouraging the Excellent* (New York: The Fund for the Advancement of Education, 1960), p. 13.

that most students will spend four years in school and that something special should be done for the more able and the more ambitious student in both the high school and the college. "Indeed, one of the best definitions of the plan is that it is a joint effort to stimulate the best students and so strengthen American Education."[8]

Despite the reservations, and in some cases, the objections of some of the colleges, the idea of advanced placement has caught on. Witness the fact that in 1956, the initial year of the Board's sponsorship, 1200 students from 104 secondary schools took 2200 examinations and went to 130 colleges; in 1961, 13,000 students from 1,100 secondary schools took 17,000 examinations and went to more than 600 colleges. Conant calls the success of the Advanced Placement Program "one of the most encouraging signs of real improvement in our educational system."[9]

One important and obvious outcome of a program of this kind is the increasing cooperation between the school and the college teachers in the several subject-matter fields covered by the program. There are eleven courses available to the secondary school on the college level: Mathematics (Calculus and Analytic Geometry), American History, French, Intermediate and Advanced German, Latin 4 and 5, English Composition, Literature, European History, Biology, Chemistry, Physics, and Spanish. The descriptions and examinations for the courses are written by a committee composed of college professors and high school teachers. Each summer there are subject matter conferences in which the professors and the high school teachers are able to meet and to discuss the subjects and to learn more about the objectives and the value of the advanced placement program. In some cases college professors have worked and taught in the high school in order to get a working knowledge of the interests and abilities of high school seniors.[10]

There seems to be some rationale for the continuing growth and the increase of activities of the Advanced Placement Programs. Angermann[11] cites several reasons why this is so. In the first place, the

---

[8]Jack N. Arbolino, "More Flies Should Practice Law," *Journal of Secondary Education*, XXXVII (April, 1962), p. 246.

[9]James B. Conant, *Slums and Suburbs* (New York: McGraw-Hill Book Company, 1961), p. 92.

[10]For example, see E. Fenton, "Working with the High School: A Professor's Testimony," *High Points*, XLIII (June, 1961), 5-15.

[11]George Angermann, "Advanced Placement, Present and Future," *National Association of Secondary School Principals' Bulletin*, XLV (November, 1961), 50-51.

standards for college admission have been raised in recent years. Many students will be convinced that in their attempt to attain entrance into the college of their choice, advanced preparation will gain for them some advantage at the admissions office. This, in effect, will attract more able students to attempt the advanced courses. Secondly, more support is expected from state councils of education and state departments of instruction. In New York, recently, the state department authorized $75,000 to subsidize summer institutes to train teachers for advanced placement instruction, with future plans to include a doubling of that amount. It is further expected that other state offices will follow suit in a similar pattern or program to encourage the Advanced Placement Program. With state support the program should continue to flourish. A third development is that the idea of special programs for the gifted is no longer thought of as undemocratic. Many school districts have budgeted money providing for special programs for the academically talented. At the state level, one legislature had been contemplating legislation which would enable the state agency to assist local boards of education financially in setting up and continuing the support of programs for the superior student. A fourth reason, according to Angermann, why the impetus for the Advanced Placement Program is likely to continue is increased interest and fuller participation on the part of the colleges. In the early years of the Advanced Placement Program few colleges endorsed or supported it with any kind of enthusiasm or vigor, but now college teachers have given it the endorsement necessary for its perpetuation. And lastly, the statement by Conant that fifteen per cent of students should be in the advanced programs, will undoubtedly stimulate further interest.

Problems and Prospects

While there are some obvious benefits and advantages to the program of Advanced Placement there are some certain disadvantages which are the peculiar problems of the college. One of the basic weaknesses is that the program itself cannot assure the continuing opportunity for advanced work or acceleration as the student moves through college. And there have been considerable differences in the way various colleges have administered Advanced Placement programs. Some have allowed Advanced Placement standing, which in fact does not shorten the time in college. Others, and this seems to be the trend, offer Advanced Placement *and* college credit. But even if placement and credit are given to the superior student, the colleges must provide a continuing selection of opportunities if the earlier successes of the program are to be realized.

Another question which must be answered is what to do with the student who, having completed the Advanced Placement courses, does not elect to apply for credit or for placement. If these courses are repeated in college it would not only seem to be a waste of time and a duplication of effort, but also would be antithetical to the main purpose of the Advanced Placement Program.

Training and selecting teachers for these students is an area of deep professional concern which needs to be considered if the overall effect of the program is to be beneficial. It means that teacher training institutions will have to re-examine their programs and formulate new goals and objectives.

In the large comprehensive high school the guidance and counselling departments have a responsibility to see that the brighter students bound for college will be enrolled in the advanced courses, while at the same time directing those students away from courses for which they are not qualified.

> The Advanced Placement Program has stimulated an appraisal of the program of studies at all levels—the elementary, secondary, and higher education. This examination and searching of the educational enterprise may well produce desirable improvements and a balance of opportunities for all of our young people.[12]

The use of College Board programs has grown substantially over the years. Table 7 below summarizes this growth as reflected in seven programs. It should be noted that the total column refers to the number of exams given, not necessarily to the number of different individuals tested. A single student might have been involved in several different programs.

If the sheer number of students who annually take the tests offered by the College Board is any indication of the influence it exerts in secondary education, one must readily conclude it is influential indeed. If the amount of "coaching" materials on the commercial market—those which "guarantee" ultimate success in the Board's examinations—is any indication of the College Board's influence with parents as well as educators, one must conclude that it is influential indeed. If the fact that colleges have been literally forced to accept

---

[12] J. J. Gerich and K. W. Lund, "How Can the Advanced Placement Program Benefit Qualified Students," *National Association of Secondary School Principals' Bulletin*, XLIV (April, 1960), 216.

TABLE 7
EDUCATIONAL TESTING SERVICE PROGRAMS CONDUCTED FOR THE COLLEGE ENTRANCE EXAMINATION BOARD, 1947-1961.*

Year	Scholastic Aptitude Test	Achievement Tests	Advanced Placement Examinations	College Scholarship Service	Preliminary Scholastic Aptitude Test	Tests Writing Sample	Total
1947-48	68,185	34,670					102,885
1948-49	68,456	34,262					102,718
1949-50	69,515	35,769					105,284
1950-51	69,446	35,531					104,977
1951-52	81,646	39,142					120,788
1952-53	94,215	44,109					138,324
1953-54	118,069	52,448	959				171,476
1954-55	115,191	71,043	1,522				187,756
1955-56	209,772	87,911	2,119				299,802
1956-57	270,291	88,295	3,772	75,654			438,012
1957-58	379,674	112,870	6,800	86,365			590,709
1958-59	473,210	137,060	8,212	86,130			716,710
1959-60	574,368	172,154	10,531	125,746	622,982		1,521,033
1960-61	732,843	241,307	13,283	165,551	733,923	88,008	1,993,068

*Sources: Educational Testing Service, *Annual Report 1960-61* (Princeton, N. J., 1961), pp. 56-57; Frank H. Bowles, "Admission to College: A Perspective for the 1960's," *Fifty-Seventh Report of the President, College Entrance Examination Board* (New York: College Entrance Examination Board, 1960), p. 12.

the Advanced Placement Programs courses for credit or placement is any indication of its effect in higher education, one must say that it is effective indeed. If the fact that the CEEB has brought about curricular changes in the comprehensive high school by the successful introduction of the Advanced Placement Courses is any indication of its impact on the secondary school, one must conclude that impact of the CEEB is great indeed.

The Impact on Public High Schools

Stanley Ptak
Robert Bunnell

Chapter 7

In order to assess the impact of the influences noted in the preceding chapters, a questionnaire study was conducted under the auspices of the Midwest Administration Center of the University of Chicago. Following the lead of the case studies reported in chapter two of this monograph, the investigators sought to test further some of the findings of that preliminary investigation. The population was expanded to include the public high schools of Illinois. Junior high schools were not part of this investigation. Data were gathered during April and May of 1962.

Four of the original eight purported nationalizing influences were considered. These were the National Science Foundation, the National Defense Education Act of 1958, the College Entrance Examination Board, and the National Merit Scholarship Program. The purpose of this investigation was to assess the nature and extent of the impact of these four selected nationalizing influences on the public secondary schools of one state. Illinois provided a wide range of schools which could be studied on the basis of three selected variables: socio-economic level, location, and size. Of the 556 public secondary schools contacted, responses from 240 or 43 per cent were received in time for use in the investigation.

To differentiate between the schools on the basis of socio-economic level, the occupational groups most representative in the high school community were used as an index. An adaptation of one of the Warner, Meeker, Eells techniques was used.[1]

Respondents were asked to indicate, in rank order of prevalence, the three most representative occupational groups in the high school

---

[1] William Lloyd Warner, Marchin Meeker, and Kenneth Eells, *Social Class in America* (Chicago: Science Research Associates, 1949), pp. 140-41.

community. A scale of seven groups was presented for their selection. The groups were as follows:
1. professionals, proprietors of large businesses or farms, major executives of large businesses;
2. semi-professionals, lower officials of large businesses;
3. office and sales employees;
4. skilled workers, craftsmen, farm foremen;
5. proprietors of small businesses or small farms;
6. semi-skilled workers, protective workers, service workers (except domestic servants);
7. unskilled workers, farm laborers, domestic servants.

To arrive at three socio-economic levels (I, II, and III—from highest to lowest), a weight of three was given to the rank order number of the most prevalent group in the community as perceived by the respondent; a weight of two to the next; and a weight of one to the respondent's third choice. In cases where one choice was made, a weight of six was assigned to that choice; in the case of two choices, the first choice received a weight of three and the second choice a weight of three. If more than three choices were made, choices beyond three were ignored. The 240 socio-economic level scores were then arranged in rank order from lowest to highest, with low scores indicating high socio-economic level, and the high scores indicating low socio-economic level. The clustering of the scores permitted the division of the sample into three classes: SEL I (high), 78 cases; SEL II (middle), 91 cases; and SEL III (low), 71 cases.

Following U. S. Bureau of Census data, five location categories were selected. These were "Rural" (population under 2,500); "Urban" (population over 2,500 but not in one of the next two categories); "Suburban" (locations on the periphery of the large metropolitan center); "Chicago" (large metropolitan center); "Total Urban" (includes urban, suburban, and Chicago categories). Applying the location categories to the sample yielded the following distribution: Rural, 121 cases; Urban, 70 cases; Suburban, 20 cases; Chicago, 29 cases; and Total Urban, 119 cases.

Three categories of school size were used. Size one schools were those up to 199 in student population; Size two those from 200-799; and Size three those 800 and above. There were 88 schools of Size one; 80 of Size two; and 72 of Size three.

The instrument used for collecting the data was a five-part questionnaire requesting 85 items of information. One section was devoted

The Impact on Public High Schools

to each of the four nationalizing influences studied. A fifth section sought general information. Most items required only a simple check-off or short answer reply. Respondents had an opportunity to express reactions and perceptions in anecdotal form, and a number of these comments appear in this chapter.

In general, there were two types of questions. One requested data dealing with the participation in various phases of the national programs; the other was concerned with respondents' perceptions of the value or usefulness of the programs to their schools.

The questionnaires were sent to the superintendents of Illinois school districts maintaining high schools. In many cases the instrument was forwarded to the principals for completion. Superintendents and principals are, therefore, the chief respondents. Findings will be reported in terms of the four nationalizing influences investigated and according to the variables of socio-economic level, location and size.

The tables presenting data according to size are arranged to consider variations which may be attributable to the size differential. The rural (size 1 and size 2) and urban (size 2 and size 3) categories were selected because there were a sufficient number of cases from which inferences might be made.

The National Science Foundation

Information was requested as to whether any present staff members had attended one or more NSF Regular Term or Summer Institutes. Respondents were also asked to report data concerning the kinds of modifications in courses of study that were made as a result of participation by the staff in NSF institutes and curriculum programs. The modifications of interest were those involving content, year courses were offered, sequence of offerings, addition of courses, or deletion of courses. Tables 8, 9, 10, and 11 summarize the findings for the National Science Foundation.

Participation in science institute programs was higher at all socio-economic levels than that of mathematics institutes, but a definite pattern may be noted as one examines participation in schools of Socio-Economic Levels I, II, and III as shown in Table 8; the *higher* the socio-economic level, the *greater* the participation.

A similar pattern appeared in the data dealing with curricular changes involving some alteration of content of courses. With respect to the addition of courses, identical percentages were found in both

TABLE 8

THE NATIONAL SCIENCE FOUNDATION PROGRAMS: PARTICIPATION AND EFFECTS REPORTED BY ILLINOIS PUBLIC HIGH SCHOOLS (PERCENTAGES REPORTED BY SOCIO-ECONOMIC LEVEL: N-240).[2]

Socio-Economic Level	N	MATHEMATICS Content Changed*	MATHEMATICS Courses Added	MATHEMATICS Institutes (one or more teachers)*	SCIENCE Content Changed*	SCIENCE Courses Added*	SCIENCE Institutes (one or more teachers)*
I	78	45	27	73	53	30	79
II	91	34	27	53	40	30	58
III	71	24	8	35	18	4	46

[2]Chi Square tables were constructed for each category of participation and effect, an asterisk indicates those categories (columns) where differences were found to be significant at the .01 level.

SEL I and SEL II in math and science. In contrast, only a small percentage of SEL III schools reported additions.

Although there were fewer reports of change in the year courses were offered, sequence of offerings, and deletion of courses, the pattern of greater change at higher socio-economic levels was discerned here also.

In the analysis by location in the category of teacher institutes again participation in science institutes was uniformly higher in all locations, with the difference being most pronounced in the rural group; 50 per cent of the schools reported participation in science, 32 per cent in math as shown in Table 9. High participation (90 per cent in science and 85 per cent in math) was reported by the suburban schools, and the urban schools (science 84 per cent, math 74 per cent). Chicago schools reported participation at the rate of 59 per cent in science and 45 per cent in math.

In the curricular areas, the suburban schools again were highest in content changes reported with 75 per cent in math and 60 per cent in science. For urban schools, 46 per cent reported content changes in math and 48 per cent in science. About a third of the Chicago schools reported changes in both science and math resulting from NSF participation; and in the rural group, slightly more schools reported changes in science than in math, but changes were reported by less than 30 per cent of these schools.

In terms of courses added, the urban schools reported the highest percentage of added courses attributable to NSF participation by

TABLE 9

THE NATIONAL SCIENCE FOUNDATION PROGRAMS: PARTICIPATION AND EFFECTS REPORTED BY ILLINOIS PUBLIC HIGH SCHOOLS (PERCENTAGES REPORTED BY LOCATION: N-240).[3]

Location	N	MATHEMATICS Content Changed*	Courses Added	Institutes (one or more teachers)*	SCIENCE Content Changed	Courses Added	Institutes (one or more teachers)
Rural	121	21	14	32	28	16	50
Urban	70	46	36	74	48	34	84
Suburban	20	75	25	85	60	30	90
Chicago	29	34	17	45	34	3	59
Total Urban	119	44	29	69	47	26	79

[3] As in Table 8, and all the following tables in this chapter, those rows or columns marked with an asterisk contain differences significant at the .01 level based on appropriate Chi Square Tests.

faculty members (36 per cent in math and 34 per cent in science). In the Chicago schools, 17 per cent reported added courses in math; but only 3 per cent reported added courses in science.

In considering the variable of size within specific locations, for institutes, 22 per cent more schools of size two in rural locations reported teachers attending math institutes than were reported in size one schools. In science there was a difference of 31 per cent. Three times as many reported added courses in math in the size two schools and four times as many in science. Content change percentages were also higher in size two schools as shown in Table 10.

In the urban schools (size two and three) a similar general pattern existed with higher percentages of size three than size two schools reporting participation in institutes, course content changes and added courses. There was not much difference in the percentages reporting science institute participants; both percentages were high.

When asked to judge the over-all effect of the NSF programs on their school, the majority responded with the rather noncommittal "some effect" reply. In the socio-economic level breakdown, SEL I had the highest "great effect" response with 28 per cent, whereas SEL III had the highest "little or no effect" response with 28 per cent. In the location breakdown, Chicago had the highest "little or no effect" judgment of NSF with 31 per cent; the 35 per cent reported by the

TABLE 10

THE NATIONAL SCIENCE FOUNDATION PROGRAMS: PARTICIPATION AND EFFECTS REPORTED BY ILLINOIS PUBLIC HIGH SCHOOLS (PERCENTAGES REPORTED BY SIZE WITHIN SPECIFIC LOCATIONS: N-191)

Location	Size	N	MATHEMATICS Content Changed*	Courses Added*	Institutes (one or more teachers)*	SCIENCE Content Changed	Courses Added*	Institutes (one or more teachers)*
Rural	1	88	16	9	26	23	9	42
	2	33	36	27	48	42	36	73
Urban	2	44	41	25	68	41	25	84
	3	26	53	54	85	61	50	85

suburban schools was the highest in the "great effect" group as shown in Table 11.

In the general anecdotal comments, we found a range of pros and cons concerning the NSF programs. A respondent in a large, SEL I

TABLE 11

THE NATIONAL SCIENCE FOUNDATION PROGRAMS: JUDGMENTS OF EFFECTS ON SCHOOL (PERCENTAGES REPORTED BY SOCIO-ECONOMIC LEVEL, SIZE, AND LOCATION)

Classification		Little or No Effect	Some Effect	Great Effect	No Response
SEL	I	16	44	28*	12
	II	25	44	13	18
	III	31	32	8	32
Size	Rural 1	28	26	7	36
	Rural 2	18	58	12	12
	Urban 2	18	57	16	9
	Urban 3	19	38	35	8
Location	Rural	27	35	8*	30
	Urban	18	50	23	9
	Suburban	0	55	35	10
	Chicago	31	31	24	14
	Total Urban	18	46	26	10

suburban school commented: "The science courses have been altered to a great extent in content; that is, materials have been added. Methods have also undergone some changes. For example, lecture-demonstrations have been changed to lab courses."

A respondent in a small, SEL III rural school wrote:

> NSF curriculum program had a positive influence upon our science offerings. One of our junior high teachers who has participated in NSF course work strengthened our science program in those grades and now teaches more there than most high school general science programs. As a direct result, we will be able to offer biology to freshmen and delete the general science.

On the other hand, some were critical or minimized the importance of NSF.

A respondent in a medium-sized, SEL III urban school wrote:

> It is the feeling here at our school that the project is poorly organized as far as the awarding of fellowships. Some teachers receive as many as three different fellowships, while others who are more in need cannot receive their first opportunity. It is my feeling the directors are more concerned with their institute and its overall advancement than the overall benefit of the fellowship.

And a respondent in a middle-sized, SEL I urban school commented: "We were working on curricular programs prior to NSF and shall continue to do so with or without the NSF."

Finally, there was this ironic touch from a small, SEL III rural school: "We have been unable to participate. Two years ago one of our teachers received an NSF scholarship and left our system."

The National Defense Education Act

Information was requested concerning present staff members who had attended one or more NDEA Summer or Regular Term Institutes in foreign language or in guidance. Information about the areas for which equipment had been purchased or remodeling accomplished with the assistance of NDEA funds was requested. Again, as in the NSF section, information was sought regarding changes in courses of study or programs that had been made as a result of increased staff, additional equipment or remodeling available through NDEA assistance. These changes were in content, year course offered, sequence of offerings, addition of courses, and deletion of courses.

In the analysis by socio-economic level shown in Table 12, in the area of added equipment and remodeling resulting from NDEA assist-

92 Nationalizing Influences on Secondary Education

ance, there was a uniformly high participation reported; about three-fourths in all three levels participated. In language equipment purchasing, the pattern of greater use at higher levels appeared again; in guidance there was no significant difference between levels in degree of participation.

In terms of curriculum, course content changes attributable to

TABLE 12

THE NATIONAL DEFENSE EDUCATION ACT: PARTICIPATION AND EFFECTS REPORTED BY ILLINOIS PUBLIC HIGH SCHOOLS (PERCENTAGES REPORTED BY SOCIO-ECONOMIC LEVEL)

Classification		Socio-Economic Levels		
		I	II	III
Science	Equipment and/or remodeling	74	76	75
	Course content changed	42	50	27
Math	Equipment and/or remodeling	50	53	28
	Course content changed	33	38	18
Language	Equipment and/or remodeling*	60	54	30
	Course content changed	36	31	14
	Fellowships (one or more teachers)*	49	32	11
Guidance	Equipment and/or remodeling	70	60	63
	Program changed*	28	27	4
	Fellowships (one or more teachers)	40	35	17

NDEA assistance in procuring equipment or remodeling were reported highest in SEL II in science and math (50 per cent and 38 per cent respectively). In language, the SEL I percentage of 36 per cent was not significantly higher than that of SEL II; and in guidance virtually the same participation was reported. However, SEL III con-

TABLE 13

THE NATIONAL DEFENSE EDUCATION ACT: PARTICIPATION AND EFFECTS REPORTED BY ILLINOIS PUBLIC HIGH SCHOOLS (PERCENTAGES REPORTED BY LOCATION)

Classification		Location				
		Rural	Urban	Suburban	Chicago	Total Urban
Science	Equipment and/or remodeling	68	76	80	100	82
	Course content changed	33	51	50	52	51
Math	Equipment and/or remodeling*	26	51	55	96	63
	Course content changed	21	39	30	52	40
Language	Equipment and/or remodeling*	24	65	90	83	74
	Course content changed*	13	37	70	41	44
	Fellowships (one or more teachers)*	13	43	85	41	50
Guidance	Equipment and/or remodeling	67	74	80	65	73
	Program changed	21	37	40	28	29
	Fellowships (one or more teachers)*	13	49	49	45	50

tent change percentages were the lowest reported; they ranged from 27 per cent in science to 4 per cent in guidance.

In teacher fellowships, both language and guidance, the pattern indicating higher participation in the higher SEL's was again evident, with the difference reaching significance in the case of language fellowships.

NDEA participation by location shown in Table 13 indicates that the gap between rural and total urban percentages was not great in science or guidance equipment and remodeling, but in math and languages the differences were significant.

Noteworthy were the high percentages of participation reported by the Chicago schools with 100 per cent in science, 96 per cent in math and 83 per cent in language. The suburban schools reported high percentages in science (80 per cent), language (90 per cent), and guidance (80 per cent). The urban high percentages appear in science (76 per cent) and guidance (74 per cent).

In the curricular area, about half of the urban schools of all types reported course content changes in science while a third in the rural schools reported such changes. Course content changes in math were highest (52 per cent) in Chicago, lowest in the rural schools (21 per cent). In language, the course content changes in suburban schools were the highest with 70 per cent; the lowest were the rural schools with 13 per cent. Program changes in guidance showed no exceptional highs, but suburban schools still maintained the highest percentage reporting such changes.

In the analysis by size shown in Table 14, the larger units, without exception, reported higher percentages of participation in all categories.

The differences were most evident between urban size two and size three in the areas of teacher fellowships (73 per cent—25 per cent in language) and (61 per cent—41 per cent in guidance); and between rural size one and size two in science remodeling (88 per cent —60 per cent) and language remodeling (45 per cent—16 per cent).

The report of judgments of the effect of NDEA on the schools is shown in Table 15. In spite of the differences in reported participation and utilization, *no* significant differences appeared in the judgments of effect.

The anecdotal comments written in the NDEA section of the questionnaire far outnumbered those related to the other national pro-

TABLE 14

THE NATIONAL DEFENSE EDUCATION ACT: PARTICIPATION AND EFFECTS REPORTED BY ILLINOIS PUBLIC HIGH SCHOOLS (PERCENTAGES REPORTED BY SIZE WITHIN SPECIFIC LOCATIONS)

Classification		Rural Size 1	Rural Size 2	Urban Size 2	Urban Size 3
Science	Equipment and/or remodeling	60	88	75	77
	Course content changed	29	42	43	54
Math	Equipment and/or remodeling*	22	36	48	58
	Course content changed	18	30	34	46
Language	Equipment and/or remodeling*	16	45	59	77
	Course content changed*	9	24	32	46
	Fellowships (one or more teachers)*	12	15	25	73
Guidance	Equipment and/or remodeling	53	61	70	81
	Program changed	17	30	23	31
	Fellowships (one or more teachers)*	11	18	41	61

grams. Although most comments were favorable, some attacks were leveled against the NDEA.

The new opportunities made possible in science were noted by a number of respondents. For example; a respondent in a small SEL

TABLE 15

THE NATIONAL DEFENSE EDUCATION ACT: JUDGMENTS OF EFFECTS ON SCHOOL
(PERCENTAGES REPORTED BY SOCIO-ECONOMIC LEVEL, SIZE, AND LOCATION)

Classification		Little or No Effect	Some Effect	Great Effect	No Response
SEL	I	14	54	28	4
	II	23	31	37	9
	III	21	31	28	20
Size	Rural 1	28	32	24	16
	Rural 2	18	39	34	9
	Urban 2	9	50	39	2
	Urban 3	27	35	23	15
Location	Rural	26	34	26	14
	Urban	16	44	33	7
	Suburban	20	50	25	5
	Chicago	7	27	45	21
	Total	14	41	35	10

III rural school wrote, "Future plans call for equipment to individualize chemistry lab work." Another school in the same category reported, "By the addition of science equipment this year, the physics course was added to our curriculum."

A suburban school noted: "Future plans include remodeling for Physical Science IX so that a lab course can be taught. In addition, biology equipment purchases will enable us to make the transition to AIBS biology plans." Another suburban school reported:

> We have been able to enrich the courses we were already teaching and have been able to add botany and zoology to the curriculum. Science has been the major field helped by NDEA. We are adding a sophomore chemistry course and moving toward an advanced placement program due to the possibility of financing additional equipment and labs.

A respondent in a middle-sized, SEL III urban school reported that they increased the counselor's time from nine to ten months as a result of NDEA assistance. However, several respondents were quite critical of this phase of the program. One respondent in a rural school wrote:

We have teachers who would like to attend, but there are too many restrictions. This program does not seem to be designed to help the smaller schools. Most of the guidance programs require an M.A. degree in that field. This is a limiting factor. Since guidance is required in all schools, it would seem plausible to open these programs to people who need the training.

And in the same vein a respondent from a middle-sized, SEL III urban school commented:

Qualification too strait-jacketed to allow us to qualify further. Total guidance set-up seemingly ignored, and eligibility made entirely contingent upon pupil-counselor ratio. This to us frustrated the purposes of the act, i.e., those that have poorest programs cannot qualify; those with the best get the most assistance.

Finally, a complaint previously noted in the NSF section was repeated: "As soon as they (our teachers) get experience and training they leave for greener pastures."

The College Entrance Examination Board

In Tables 16 through 19, which summarize the data, the heading "Some form of special preparation" refers to that kind of activity on the part of the school over and above routine announcements and record keeping. It involved such activities as special classes, orientation sessions, or coaching.

First, regarding CEEB participation in terms of socio-economic level, the frequently noted pattern of significantly higher participation by schools of high SEL was again clearly discernible here in nearly all aspects: application for membership, attendance at meetings and advanced placement programs. Only the differences in the last row of Table 16 were not significant.

In Table 17 the clearly evident leadership of the suburban schools was noted with 75 per cent applying for membership, 75 per cent reporting staff members in attendance at meetings, and 65 per cent with one or more Advanced Placement programs. Chicago, however, reported the highest percentage of schools giving some form of special preparation (48 per cent).

In the breakdown by size within specific locations reported in Table 18, the variation was slight, and followed the pattern of the larger the school the greater the participation. Participation in CEEB programs was light in all four categories.

In the judgment of the influence of CEEB as reported in Table 19, the over-all reaction was that CEEB had little influence on the

TABLE 16

THE COLLEGE ENTRANCE EXAMINATION BOARD: PARTICIPATION AND PREPARATION REPORTED BY ILLINOIS PUBLIC HIGH SCHOOLS (PERCENTAGES REPORTED BY SOCIO-ECONOMIC LEVEL)

Classification	Socio-Economic Level		
	I	II	III
Applied for CEEB membership*	32	17	10
Staff members attended CEEB meetings*	36	12	6
Utilize one or more advanced placement programs*	37	22	11
Utilize some form of special preparation	27	24	11

school's curriculum. The highest percentage noted was the 45 per cent of the suburban schools, but no significant differences were found. The actions reported in Tables 16, 17, and 18 were of a considerably higher order than the reported effects. For example, 65 per cent of the suburban schools utilized Advanced Placement programs, but only 50 per cent indicated a noticeable influence on curriculum.

TABLE 17

THE COLLEGE ENTRANCE EXAMINATION BOARD: PARTICIPATION AND PREPARATION REPORTED BY ILLINOIS PUBLIC HIGH SCHOOLS (PERCENTAGES REPORTED BY LOCATION)

Classification	Location				
	Rural	Urban	Suburban	Chicago	Total Urban
Applied for CEEB membership*	13	17	75	17	27
Staff members attended CEEB meetings*	2	21	75	34	34
Utilize one or more Advanced Placement program*	12	24	65	41	35
Utilize some form of special preparation*	11	23	35	48	31

The Impact on Public High Schools

TABLE 18
THE COLLEGE ENTRANCE EXAMINATION BOARD: PARTICIPATION AND PREPARATION REPORTED BY ILLINOIS PUBLIC HIGH SCHOOLS
(PERCENTAGES REPORTED BY SIZE WITHIN SPECIFIC LOCATIONS)

Classification	Rural Size 1	Rural Size 2	Urban Size 2	Urban Size 3
Applied for CEEB membership	13	12	7	35
Staff members attended CEEB meetings*	1	6	18	27
Utilize one or more Advanced Placement programs	11	15	18	35
Utilize some form of special preparation	11	12	18	31

TABLE 19
THE COLLEGE ENTRANCE EXAMINATION BOARD: JUDGMENTS OF EFFECTS ON SCHOOL
(PERCENTAGES REPORTED BY SOCIO-ECONOMIC LEVEL, SIZE, AND LOCATION)

Classification		Little or No Influence	Some Influence	Great Influence	No Response
SEL	I	59	33	4	4
	II	70	18	3	9
	III	60	13	0	27
Size	Rural 1	62	14	1	23
	Rural 2	70	21	0	9
	Urban 2	70	21	2	7
	Urban 3	69	23	0	8
Location	Rural	64	16	1	19
	Urban	70	22	1	7
	Suburban	45	45	5	5
	Chicago	59	24	10	7
	Total Urban	63	26	4	7

100 Nationalizing Influences on Secondary Education

In Chicago 41 per cent of the respondents utilized Advanced Placement programs, but only about one-third of the respondents reported a noticeable effect on the curriculum.

The National Merit Scholarship Program

In a general question regarding participation in the National Merit Scholarship Program, a high percentage, as shown in Table 20, in each SEL reported such participation. In the same table virtually all respondents reported participation, when considered according to size and location of the schools. As to special preparation, again Chicago schools reported a high 69 per cent in this category, far surpassing any other group.

TABLE 20

THE NATIONAL MERIT SCHOLARSHIP PROGRAM:
PARTICIPATION AND PREPARATION
REPORTED BY ILLINOIS PUBLIC HIGH SCHOOLS
(PERCENTAGES REPORTED BY SOCIO-ECONOMIC LEVEL,
SIZE, AND LOCATION)

Classification		Participate in NMS Program	Some Form of Special Preparation
SEL	I	97	27
	II	94	30
	III	88	17
Size	Rural 1	100	19
	Rural 2	100	12
	Urban 2	100	11
	Urban 3	100	31
Location	Rural	100	17*
	Urban	100	18
	Suburban	100	30
	Chicago	91	69
	Total Urban	98	33

In Table 21 again the "little or no influence" item received the majority of responses, with 35 per cent the highest "some influence" response. While the phrase "some influence" was undoubtedly defined differently by each respondent seeing it in the scale, it would seem that there is a discrepancy between the actions reported in Table 20 and the influence reported in Table 21. If 69 per cent of the Chicago respondents employ some form of special preparation for their students, more than 31 per cent might have been expected to have reported some or great influence.

TABLE 21

THE NATIONAL MERIT SCHOLARSHIP PROGRAM: JUDGMENTS OF EFFECTS ON SCHOOL (PERCENTAGES REPORTED BY SOCIO-ECONOMIC LEVEL, SIZE, AND LOCATION)

Classification		Judgment of Influence			
		Little or No Influence	Some Influence	Great Influence	No Response
SEL	I	68	23	7	2
	II	66	26	3	5
	III	56	31	0	13
Size	Rural 1	64	26	3	7
	Rural 2	67	27	0	6
	Urban 2	66	27	2	5
	Urban 3	65	15	8	12
Location	Rural	65	26	2	7
	Urban	66	23	4	7
	Suburban	60	35	5	0
	Chicago	62	24	7	7
	Total Urban	64	25	5	6

The anecdotal comments concerning the National Merit Scholarship Program were, on the whole, negative in tone. Many of these comments seemed to indicate a feeling of greater influence than was reported on the influence scale. For example, two suburban respondents wrote: "The National Merit Scholarships are too greatly overrated by parents as a measure of the quality of the school program," and,

> We think the National Merit plan is harmful. It is geared too much toward math and science. Persons win over better students because of where their parents are employed. The public gains a false impression of the over-all caliber of the school. We have experienced these reactions.

A Chicago respondent commented:

> When we place seventeen students above the 98th percentile but earn no scholarships the word gets around that it is rather

hopeless. We receive 40 to 60 other scholarships annually, and though the amount may be small (in money) it is very encouraging.

Thus the actions of the schools and the kinds of comments made seem to indicate a greater impact of this program than the influence scale indicated.

Summary and Conclusions

The purpose of the investigation was to assess the nature and extent of the impact of four nationalizing influences on the public high schools of Illinois. The analysis was made in terms of three variables: socio-economic level of the community, size of the school, and location of the community.

Tables 8 through 11 summarized the data on the National Science Foundation. In terms of the SEL index the higher the level, the greater has been the participation in all aspects of the programs. This relationship appeared to be particularly true of the use of teacher fellowships. When considering the variable of location, it was found that the suburban and urban (other than Chicago) schools made more changes and participated more frequently than the Chicago and rural schools. It was also clear that the larger the school, the greater the participation in NSF fellowships and the greater the response in the form of course change and addition. In general the nature of the impact was broad, affecting curriculum and teacher training, and the extent of the impact varied according to SEL, size and location, with the wealthier, larger schools in the suburbs and independent cities reflecting the most influence. In general these conclusions were supported by the reported judgments of influence, although fewer schools reported a "great influence" judgment than demonstrated it in the intensity of their involvement in the programs.

Tables 12 through 15 summarized the data on the National Defense Education Act. In general the utilization of NDEA opportunities was more uniform than in the case of the National Science Foundation. All SEL's have made extensive use of equipment and remodeling funds, with the biggest difference between levels occurring in the expected area, language. The college-preparatory nature of language instruction would lead one to expect the least utilization of this program among the lowest socio-economic levels, and this was the case. More curriculum changes seemed to be made by the wealthier, larger, nonrural schools, while the utilization of the fellowships followed a pattern similar to that in the utilization of NSF Institutes. Of the four influences studied, the NDEA was seen as the most important influence by more than half of the respondents. This choice may have been influenced by the visibility of laboratories and equipment, to the exclusion of equally powerful influences on curriculum by the NSF, the College Entrance Examination Board, and the National Merit Scholarship Program.

Tables 16 through 19 summarized the data on the College Entrance Examination Board. Participation in these programs varied in the pattern expected, that is, the higher the socio-economic level of the community, the greater the participation. Variation according to location was striking, with 75 per cent of the suburban respondents reporting some participation, while only 13 per cent of the rural respondents participated in the CEEB programs. The variation according to size was as expected, but not very great. The larger the school, the greater the tendency to participate. The frequency with which influence was reported was again noticeably lower than the frequency of use of programs.

The final influence considered was the National Merit Scholarship Program. Here, participation was virtually unanimous. Judgment of influence was uniformly low, with the exception that 40 per cent of the suburban respondents reported a noticeable influence from this program, the highest percentage of any of the classifications. It was this program that received the most negative comments, usually related to the kind of invidious comparisons brought about by the publishing of the results of the annual testing.

In general terms it would appear that these four influences have had a considerable impact on the high schools studied. They have brought about changes in course content, addition of new courses, increased academic training of the teachers, additions to facilities and equipment, and introduction of special forms of preparation for the various testing programs employed. These kinds of influence, moreover, are not uniformly felt among the schools. In a number of instances it appeared that the wealthier, larger, nonrural schools were the ones that were most frequently influenced by these programs through their participation in the many opportunities offered. This differential utilization of programs, combined with the recurring discrepancy between reported influence and degree of participation can only suggest that educators, school boards, and citizens must become more aware of these influences in order to make informed decisions about participation. However, these decisions will have to be based not only on adequate information, but will have to be consistent with the philosophy that each local district is empowered, in fact required, to develop.

National Movements and Independent Schools

Roy A. Larmee | Chapter 8

The major purpose of this study was two fold: first, to examine the influence of certain national movements in education on a group of selected independent secondary schools, and second, to determine what part these schools have had in the development of the programs which make up these movements. The primary emphasis was on the schools rather than on the programs. The use of the term "national movement" refers to efforts being carried out at the national level to improve American education in specific fields such as curriculum, testing, school organization and finance. Each movement is fostered by a series of diverse groups which have developed well organized programs to carry out their objectives.

It was expected that these programs do influence national policy which in turn is effective in the determination of policy for individual independent schools. Policies, for purposes of this study, have been defined in Parson's terms as guidelines which commit the educational institution as a whole.[1] Basic policies establish the long range objectives and chart the destinies of the enterprise. Intermediate policies are developed to assist personnel in a given institution in establishing direction for each level of planning and action operating to achieve the basic goals of the institution.

The investigation of the effect of national programs upon individual school policy making could be done using either public or private secondary schools. This study focused on independent schools because of the assumption that they should be more able to depart from regional, state, or national control than public schools. The diversity of purpose represented in the whole range of American private

---

[1] Talcott Parsons, *Structure and Process in Modern Societies* (Glencoe: The Free Press, 1960), p. 30.

education made it necessary to develop a set of criteria to govern the selection of schools to be used in the study. The following criteria were developed, therefore, to govern the selection of schools:

1. That the majority of students enrolled in these secondary schools plan to enroll in colleges and universities,

2. That the schools be of good academic quality as evidenced by graduates' success in institutions of higher education,

3. That the schools have established some reputation for program innovation at the secondary level,

4. That the final selection of schools represent a wide geographical distribution.

A panel of experts was utilized to identify the schools for the investigator. The panel included twelve persons in the following categories:

1. Two university admissions officers,
2. Two independent school headmasters,
3. One president of a college of education,
4. Three officials associated with regional accrediting associations,
5. One official from a national association of independent schools,
6. One author of a recent book on the history of education,
7. One superintendent of schools, formerly an assistant headmaster of a private school and an official in a regional secondary school accrediting association,
8. One former university examiner.

Each member of the panel was asked to nominate fifteen schools which met the criteria noted above. The panel members responded by sending nomination lists which varied from three to twenty-seven schools.

A total of seventy-nine schools were nominated; the final criterion of selection used was frequency of nomination, although three exceptions were made to broaden the geographical range of the sample. The eleven sample schools and the two pilot schools were located in the following states: Connecticut, Georgia, Illinois (2), Indiana, Massachusetts, Michigan, Missouri, New Hampshire (2), New Jersey, and New York (2).

The data were gathered through the use of the focused interview with headmasters and members of their staffs and through the examination of school documents collected by the investigator. Headmaster interviews varied in length from one and one-half hours to four hours in length. All interviews were conducted by the investigator.

After the schools had been selected, a search of the literature was made to learn the names of teachers in these schools who had been involved in the ten national programs of interest in the study. Whenever possible these teachers were sought out and interviewed; other science and mathematics teachers as well as teachers assigned to other subject fields were also interviewed.[2]

Following the pilot interviews, changes were made in the interview guides and in the list and type of potential school documents to be collected. A set of empirical codes was developed for data drawn from documents as well as teacher and headmaster interviews. These were applied consistently to data obtained from all of the schools. The unit of analysis used in the coding was the school, and new codes were established to take account of the data which were unanticipated. All materials were hand-coded in a manner that permitted data obtained from headmaster and teacher interviews, school documents and other sources to be used to answer specific questions posed in the study. There were thirty-eight questions in the headmaster interview guide and ten questions in the teacher guide. The responses to questions in the headmaster guide were combined with teacher interview and documentary data. These data were then grouped in terms of their relevance to the following four basic questions of the study.

1. How do the eleven independent schools define their role and purpose, or in other words, what is their stated role in American education?

2. What part, if any, have these schools had in the determination of the direction and scope of the ten national programs enumerated below?

3. How do these national programs affect the formulation and reformulation of goals in the eleven schools?

4. To what extent have the eleven schools carried on local independent innovation in the areas covered by the national movements, i.e., science and mathematics, and in other areas such as social studies and English.

Reliability of the coding was established by the use of three coders —the investigator and two Midwest Administration Center staff asso-

---

[2]Science and mathematics teachers were especially sought because the five national curriculum programs all were active in these two fields.

ciates who had had previous administrative experience. The staff associates coded all responses to a selected group of the most difficult interview questions. The resultant coefficients of correlation exceeded .83.

The Programs

The ten national programs included in the study were made up of: two external testing programs—The College Entrance Examination Board and the National Merit Scholarship program; five curriculum revision programs—the Physical Science Study Committee, the School Mathematics Study Group, the Biological Sciences Curriculum Study, the Chemical Education Material Study, and the Chemical Bond Approach Project; and three programs under titles of the National Defense Education Act—Titles III, V, and VI. A survey of the literature revealed certain similarities and differences in the programs in terms of areas of interest, organization, patterns of support and in procedures used to develop the programs.

Areas of similar interest to all ten program groups included: the subject matter fields of science and mathematics, and the able college-bound student. Leaders of nine of the ten programs displayed a common interest in the improvement of curriculum or guidance programs, while eight of the ten programs concentrated some of their efforts on evaluation and testing.

The organization of these national groups was found to be similar in a number of ways. While their efforts were concentrated in the area of education, their central advisory or steering groups are drawn from wide professional backgrounds which include: college and university administrators and faculty members, secondary school teachers and administrators, representatives of business and industry, publishers, film producers, communication specialists, and representatives of professional organizations.

Differences were also found in the organizational structure of the groups. The outstanding difference was that presented by the National Defense Education Act with its combination of administrative organizations at the federal and state levels. Two other groups, the College Entrance Examination Board and the National Merit Scholarship Program, were found to engage the services of other agencies to assist them in developing and carrying out their programs.

Some similarities were discovered in the procedures followed by the program groups. The organizers of the five curriculum groups

National Movements and Independent Schools 109

used writing teams to develop their programs, engaged large numbers of schools in the experimental phases of development, and used the services of one testing agency to assist them in the evaluation of their programs.

Procedural differences were most evident in the three Titles of the National Defense Education Act. State level plans had to be submitted in some cases before local schools could receive funds, while in other cases direct negotiations were made between the U. S. Office of Education and the local schools. In the curriculum groups there were procedural differences, too, in the type and number of courses developed and in the way in which provisions were made for publication of their materials.

Financial support for the programs was recognized as coming from both public and private sources. Primary support for the two testing programs came from private funds while the other eight programs received their major support from National Science Foundation and from federal funds appropriated to support the National Defense Education Act. One of these federal sources has also provided some support for one of the testing services, thus nine of the ten programs have received some support from federal funds.

In synthesizing these findings a number of factors may be noted. Each of the ten programs was seen as a national program in that its support was not provided by a state or regional agency but by national agencies either public or private. All of the programs designed by these groups were reported to be available for use in all parts of the country. The experimental phases of the programs have been carried out on a national scale also; this was particularly evident in the development of the five curriculum groups. The national character of the programs was also revealed by the fact that the central advisory or steering groups were drawn from all parts of the country, as well as from a wide range of institutions. An examination of the findings also indicated that arrangements to participate in nine of the ten programs had been made directly between the national groups and the local educational agency without the approval of any intervening level of government or other public or private agency.

Although some very basic changes in national programs were developed by the ten groups included in the study, this experimentation and change was rapidly accepted by a large number of school systems across the country. In one of the curriculum programs (the Biological Sciences Curriculum Study) the second year's experimental group numbered more than 50,000 students in thirty-five states. In another (the Physical Science Study Committee) it was estimated that at the end of five years 20 per cent of U. S. high school students taking physics had used this course.[3] In the past six years the testing services have also experienced rapid periods of growth in terms of the number of secondary school students using their examination services.

The common areas of interest noted earlier were supplemented by evidences of complex sets of interrelationships. All five of the curriculum groups used the same testing agency to assist them in evaluating their programs. One of the testing programs (National Merit Scholarship Corporation) for example, required that test results on the National Merit test be substantiated by scores on another examination. All of the 1961 Merit winners also took the College Board examination. The testing provisions of the National Defense Education Act also provided support for examinations developed by one of the two testing programs in the study.

The Schools and the Programs

The major focus of this study was on eleven independent secondary schools, and specifically on their relationship to the national programs included in the study. The findings indicate the relationship of the ten national programs to the policies and goals of the schools.

Purposes of the Schools

In order to establish a relationship between the programs and the schools, it was necessary to determine whether there were purposes common to the eleven schools. Two basic purposes were found to be common to all the schools. These were: the provision of a school program that would prepare all students for entrance into college following graduation from secondary school; and the provision of a sound, challenging and valuable academic program. These two goals and their implementing policies were examined to determine whether there was a relationship between the goals and the national programs considered in the study.

The headmasters' perception of the criteria which were regarded as being important by college admissions officers became important. A universally perceived requirement was the compilation of a sound

---

[3] Ervin H. Hofforth, "Physical Science Study Committee," *Science Education News* (December, 1961), 4.

academic record by the student applicant. Six of the headmasters felt that the single most important criterion in determining the academic competence of a student as viewed by admissions officers were the students' scores on the College Entrance Examination tests. Thus these tests were a means of evaluating the extent to which students attained program goals. Four of the five remaining headmasters felt that the school's recommendation was the most important criterion for admission among colleges "that know us," but that among the increasing number of colleges that did not know them, the College Board scores were regarded as the most important criterion.

The Testing Programs

An analysis of the data indicated that both the College Entrance Examination Board and the National Merit Scholarship programs were offered in all of the schools included in the study. Headmasters did not feel that the National Merit program had any effect on the goals of the schools. An examination of the College Board programs revealed quite a different situation. These programs were found to be the greatest single influence on the policies of the schools. Every school provided examples of curriculum policies which were designed to prepare students to take the Advanced Placement examinations although the number of fields in which these examinations were given varied from school to school. Satisfactory passage of one of these tests became a curriculum goal in each one of the schools.

Satisfactory passage of the other College Board tests was also found to be an important criterion relative to the college preparatory purpose of the schools as noted above. College admissions officers were reported to view College Board scores as evidence of the extent to which students presented a sound academic background and this sound academic program was, in turn, one of the two major purposes subscribed to in all of the schools.

The Five National Curriculum Programs

In the four fields covered by the five curriculum programs, policy decisions had been made by the introduction of portions of the new programs in the following number of schools in each curriculum area: physics, Physical Science Study Committee—all eleven schools, Advanced Placement—nine of the schools; mathematics, School Mathematics Study Group—four of the schools, Advanced Placement—nine of the schools; biology, Biological Sciences Study Committee—two of the schools, Advanced Placement—six of the schools; chemistry,

Chemical Bond Approach and Chemical Education Material Study—three of the schools each, and Advanced Placement—seven of the schools. When the new programs and Advanced Placement were combined in each field, curriculum policies had been changed in from seven to eleven of the schools, depending on which subject matter field was considered. A further finding was that no other new external national curriculum had been adopted by these schools in the fields of mathematics, physics, biology and chemistry.

Experimentation of some kind was being carried out in all of the schools even though only seven of the schools stated this as a major purpose. The field of greatest activity for experimentation was social studies, which was also the field identified by headmasters as most in need of revision. Support for some of this experimentation was provided from external sources, while other projects were financed exclusively by school funds.

Titles III, V, and VI of the National Defense Education Act

Headmasters indicated that none of the schools had taken advantage of any of these provisions, and thus there were no direct policy implications evident in the schools. Indirect evidence was, however, noted in headmaster interviews. Seven headmasters perceived that N.D.E.A. provided a portion of the increased support which had been given to public secondary schools. They felt this increased support had resulted in the development of more public schools which were similar in quality to those headed by these seven headmasters and that this increased support and improved quality made public schools more competitive with the independent schools. This in turn had caused the independent schools to accelerate fund drives and raise tuition. When these costs were combined with the perceived improvement of public schools, new recruiting problems for some of the independent schools were anticipated.

The Schools and Program Development

The National Merit Scholarship Program

The eleven headmasters of the schools included in the study stated that no member of their staffs had had any part in the development of the National Merit Scholarship programs. No staff member had served on any of the National Merit Committees or as a consultant to the program.

The College Entrance Examination Board

An analysis of these data revealed that participation in the development of College Board Programs had been extensive; *all* sample schools had contributed staff members to serve on one of the College Board committees. One of the newest CEEB programs (Advanced Placement) was chosen for closer examination. Two factors were considered, the origin of the program and the service in 1961 of sample school staff members on committees which assisted in the operation of this program. The original study to which Advanced Placement traces its origin was made by three secondary schools and three universities. All three secondary schools were included in the study. Teachers representing sample schools were chosen to prepare examinations for six of the eleven subject matter fields covered by the 1961 Advanced Placement examinations and twenty-six of

TABLE 22

THE INVOLVEMENT OF THE ELEVEN INDEPENDENT SCHOOLS IN THE ORIGIN OF THE ADVANCED PLACEMENT PROGRAM AND IN THE 1961 EXAMINATION AND READING COMMITTEES

Type of Involvement	1	2	3	4	5	6	7	8	9	10	11	Pilot School 1
Schools which were part of the original study which resulted in creation of Advanced Placement						*	*	*				
No. of teachers who served on Central Committee of Advanced Placement						1						
No. of teachers who served on Examination Committee of Advanced Placement						2	1	1	1			1
No. of teachers who served as readers of Advanced Placement examinations		2	2			7	4	4	3		1	3

*Schools 6, 7, and 8 were among the five most heavily endowed schools in the study, were boys' schools, and provided facilities for both boarding and day students. Enrollments (1960) ranged from 637 to 817 and of a total of 664 graduates in 1960, all but twenty-six entered college in the fall of that year.

the 237 readers of the examinations were from these schools. Only four schools in the study were not represented in the 1961 Advanced Placement Examination or reading committees. Five of the six examination committee members and fifteen of the twenty-six readers were recruited from the same three schools which made the study resulting in the origin of the Advanced Placement program as shown in Table 22.

The Five National Curriculum Programs

A total of twenty-one leadership positions for the five curriculum programs were filled by staff members from the eleven independent schools. These positions included membership on central advisory or steering committees, writing teams, and committees which developed special projects, as well as participation in the evaluation of the initial experimentation in the secondary school setting. Seventeen of these leadership positions were held by personnel drawn from the same three schools which were the major contributors to the Advanced Placement Programs. Five of the schools in the study were not represented in any of these leadership positions in the curriculum groups. Two of these schools were also in the group not represented among the schools which contributed to the 1961 Advanced Placement examination committees, as shown in Table 23.

The Three Titles of the National Defense Education Act

All headmasters of schools reported that no members of their staff had been involved in any way in the development of the programs available under Titles III, V, and VI of the National Defense Education Act. It was also found that no staff member from the schools in the study had served as a consultant to the groups which developed these programs.

Conclusions

The findings which have been presented provide evidence to support a number of conclusions.

The Programs

1. National agencies with both public and private support and drawing personnel from all geographical regions of the United States have developed national programs which have been used in all parts of the country.

TABLE 23

LEADERSHIP POSITIONS IN THE FIVE CURRICULUM PROGRAMS WHICH WERE FILLED FROM THE ELEVEN SCHOOLS*

Leadership Position	1	2	3	4	5	6	7	8	9	10	11
B.S.C.S. Steering Committee								1			
B.S.C.S. Committee on Innovations in Laboratory Instruction								1			
B.S.C.S. Summer Writing Team								1			
C.B.A. Writing Conference						1					
C.B.A. Evaluation Participants						2					
S.M.S.G. Advisory Committee								1			
S.M.S.G. Panel on Monographs								1			
S.M.S.G. Panel on Teacher Training Materials							1				
S.M.S.G. Writing Session Participants						1	2				
S.M.S.G. Panel on Programmed Learning								1			
S.M.S.G. Panel on Small Publications						1					
CHEM Study Trial Participants			1	1				1			
P.S.S.C. Central Contributing Staff							1	1			
P.S.S.C. Committee to Develop New C.E.E.B. Test to Include P.S.S.C. Physics								1			
P.S.S.C. Made Original Trial of materials								1			
Total Positions Held in Each School	0	0	1	1	2	4	6	7	0	0	0

*Figures indicate number of positions, not different individuals as some persons functioned in more than one position.

2. In a society where education is traditionally regarded as a state function, nine of the ten national programs have established direct relationships with local educational agencies without the intervention of any state or regional agency.

3. In terms of the definition of policy used throughout this study these national groups, both public and private, have succeeded in effecting change in local educational policy as their programs have been rapidly adopted by local school systems.

4. Through wide participation in the experimental phases of the curriculum programs, local educational agencies have indicated their willingness to allow student participation in nationally devised programs even though they are admittedly in the experimental or developmental phases.

5. Major support for eight of the ten programs came from funds appropriated by Congress to be spent in the national interest. These funds were used to develop programs which if adopted would result in local educational policy changes which presumably reflect the national interest.

6. The composition of the central advisory and developmental committees of the ten programs reflected broad representation of educational levels and lay leadership. These groups developed educational programs which when adopted resulted in a change in local educational policy.

7. A review of the activities of the five curriculum groups would seem to indicate that there are a number of forces which must be dealt with in effecting widespread change in secondary courses of study. Each of the five curriculum groups included among their activities the writing of textbooks, the training of teachers, and the use of a national testing agency, both to assist them in the evaluation of their programs and to develop achievement tests to determine whether students attained the objectives established for the program.

The Schools and the Programs

1. A national external testing program can be used in a school without affecting school goals. In schools in this study both of the national testing programs were used by all of the schools, but one (National Merit) was not seen as affecting local school goals by any of the headmasters.

2. The single most important criterion as to whether a student has received a sound academic education, in the eyes of the college admissions officer, is his performance on the College Entrance Examination Board tests. Six of the headmasters stated that College Board scores were the most important criterion in college admission, while four of the remaining headmasters stated that it was the most important criterion when the school is unfamiliar to the admissions officer.

3. When major changes are made in traditional curriculums, it is desirable to have the College Board examinations changed. This con-

clusion may be drawn from the fact that in the case of two of the curriculum programs it was necessary to send letters to colleges explaining the participation of applying students in the experimental phases of two of the programs. It was also interesting to note in this connection that the one program which was used in part by all of the schools was the one for which the College Board has changed its examination.

4. Of the ten programs examined in this study, the one which had the greatest effect on the policies of the eleven schools was the College Entrance Examination Board program. The Advanced Placement programs were used in at least one course in all of the schools, and the schools were major contributors of students presented for advanced placement candidacy. The College Boards were the most widely used of the ten programs considered.

5. Independent schools continue to demonstrate their independence in terms of the relationships established with the ten programs. Even though some of the schools were aware of the new programs or in some cases had even contributed leadership to the programs, other programs were chosen for use in their schools, because they suited their purposes better.

6. As the curriculum groups continue to work on courses beyond the high school level, it will be desirable to change the Advanced Placement examinations. All of the curriculum groups included provisions for the able student as part of their programs, and the most advanced programs used in the eleven schools were the Advanced Placement programs. All eleven schools were listed as Advanced Placement schools in May of 1961.

7. The rapid expansion of college level work being carried out in these schools would seem to support the conclusion that what has traditionally been regarded as college level work can be successfully mastered by at least a portion of the secondary school population. This conclusion has been supported by the examination performance of students and by the willingness of colleges to accept Advanced Placement examination scores as evidence of satisfactory mastery of the material.

8. Increased support of the public schools through public funds has posed new problems of competition for the independent schools and unless new sources of funds are uncovered, those schools which are marginal in terms of financial support will have increasing difficulty in remaining competitive with the public schools.

The Schools and Program Development

1. While each of the schools has contributed staff members to the development of some phase of the College Board programs, the vast majority of the membership of the 1961 Advanced Placement Examination and Reader Committees drawn from schools included in the study came from the same three schools which took part in the study which is credited with originating the program. Of the twenty-one leadership positions which were filled from the eleven schools, seventeen were staffed by teachers from the same three schools which contributed leadership to the Advanced Placement programs. It may therefore be concluded that although the various curriculum programs and the CEEB are structurally and organizationally independent of each other, they have tended to look to the same schools for leadership in developing their programs.

2. Two of the eleven schools failed to contribute a member to any of the program groups. Both of these schools were in the lowest category of frequency of nomination from which schools were chosen for the study. The three schools which made the greatest contribution were most frequently nominated by the "panel of experts," thus verifying the nominations.

3. The contributions of teachers from the independent schools support the conclusion that the program leaders felt that able and competent teachers could be found in these schools and that these individuals and schools would be willing to contribute the time and effort necessary to serve with these groups as a part of their responsibility to education.

4. The fact that in four of the five curriculum groups teachers served on the committees in the initial stages of development would seem to indicate they were instrumental in helping to launch the programs and had not merely "jumped on the bandwagon" once it started to roll.

The extensive participation of some of the eleven schools in six of the programs would seem to support the conclusion that certain independent schools continue to reflect, but in a new way, the innovative role which has traditionally been credited to them, but which has been challenged in some quarters recently.

Impact and Implications

Roald F. Campbell
Robert Bunnell

Chapter 9

In the preceding chapters a number of national programs which appear to be influencing secondary education were examined, and some assessment of these influences on both public and independent secondary schools was made.

But national programs in education, public and private, are too numerous for their complete description to be contained in one monograph. For instance, no consideration was given to the educational aspects of the World War II G.I. Bill of Rights which expired in 1956 after 7.8 million veterans had received educational benefits at a total cost of 14.5 billion dollars. Nor was any study made of the provisions affecting school districts in federally impacted areas for which one billion dollars was expended for construction and another billion for the operation of schools during the period 1951 to 1960. No treatment was included of the educational programs distributed among 27 major departments and agencies and 17 minor agencies in the executive branch of the federal government.[1] Nor were the decisions of the U. S. Supreme Court as they relate to education subjected to any analysis. Studies of some of these questions have been done under other auspices, other studies wait to be done.

A number of other national programs received but scant attention and that only in Chapter 2. These included the philanthropic foundations, the American Council on Testing, the various professional associations, the secondary school accrediting bodies, and numerous special interest groups which have ideological or commercial interests to "sell" to the schools. We are convinced that each of these programs ought to become the object of one or more studies.

---

[1] Charles A. Quattlebaum, *Federal Educational Policies, Programs and Proposals, Part II* (Washington: U. S. Government Printing Office, 1960).

The findings and conclusions presented in this chapter grow, for the most part, out of our examination of four national programs and their apparent impact on secondary schools. We are not unaware, however, that the nationalizing influences to which we allude may be closely related to other influences and programs at the national level. We thus encounter, as is so often the case in social action, the problem of multiple causation. The sections of our report dealing with the four programs provide considerable presumptive evidence that these programs have had an impact on secondary schools. The actual examination of practice provides evidence of this impact that is even more conclusive.

Impact

The findings of the studies reported here may be summarized in nine general statements.

1. National programs have changed substantially the courses offered in science, mathematics, and foreign languages in our high schools. In the case of science and mathematics, this has been done chiefly through the course content improvement programs and institutes for the in-service training of teachers, both sponsored by the National Science Foundation and explained in some detail in Chapter 3. In the case of foreign language, the impetus has come chiefly from the National Defense Education Act which has provided institutes for the in-service education of teachers and money for needed equipment. For purposes of illustrating the impact, the findings of Chapter 7 for the urban schools will be used to epitomize the data since the reports of the urban schools usually fell between the extremes reported by the rural schools on the one hand and the suburban schools on the other. In the urban schools, 44 per cent reported changed content in mathematics, 47 per cent in science, and 44 per cent in foreign language.

The Advanced Placement program represents another notable change in high school offerings. Beginning with an experimental program under Ford Foundation auspices in 1951, the College Entrance Examination Board assumed responsibility for the preparation of the Advanced Placement examinations in 1955. Between 1956 and 1961, schools using the examinations increased from 104 to 1,100; students taking the examinations increased from 1,200 to 13,000, and colleges accepting the examinations increased from 130 to 600. Advanced Placement examinations are now offered in eleven courses, as noted in Chapter 6, and these include not only science, mathematics, and foreign language but history and English as well. Only in this decade have high schools been permitted to offer college-level courses.

2. National programs have altered the guidance programs of our high schools. As was noted in Chapter 5, the counselor-student ratio for the high schools of the nation was changed from 1:750 to 1:610, tests administered for guidance purposes were increased from two to 19 million, and 203 guidance institutes were organized with NDEA support in 47 states during the first year of operation of the NDEA. For the urban high schools reported in Chapter 7, 73 per cent had received new equipment or remodeling of guidance facilities, 29 per cent had changed their guidance programs, and 50 per cent had had one or more teachers participate in a guidance institute. In both the approval of institute programs and the allocation of guidance materials, NDEA played a dominant role.

3. National programs have created a vast external testing program for our high schools. The National Merit Scholarship program, as noted in Chapter 4, was organized in 1955 and began testing operations in 1956. In the first year 10,000 schools and 58,000 students were involved in the examinations. By 1961 the schools had increased to 15,000 and the students to 587,000. At the outset, the program had 24 private sponsors of whom Ford and Carnegie were the chief donors, and by 1961 sponsors had grown to 133. Among the high schools reported in Chapter 7, 100 per cent of the rural high schools and 98 per cent of the urban schools had participated in the National Merit program.

With the establishment of the Educational Testing Service in 1948 and the use of ETS as the testing arm of the College Entrance Examination Board, the growth in external testing has been phenomenal. In 1947-48, ETS administered about 100,000 tests to secondary school pupils, by 1960-61 the number had grown to almost two million. CEEB, like the National Merit program, is a private venture; no school or no student is required to participate in the testing program. These programs, together with the testing programs of the American Council on Testing, serve to demonstrate, however, the power of nongovernmental agencies, sometimes called private government.

4. National programs have changed college admissions procedures. As long as CEEB was limited to a few colleges and secondary schools along the Atlantic seaboard, its influence was slight. But membership in the Board has now expanded to 427 colleges, 165 secondary schools, and 41 educational associations. As shown in Chap-

ter 6, many non-member colleges and even more non-member secondary schools are making increasing use of one or more of the services provided by the College Board. For instance, among the urban schools reported in Chapter 7, 34 per cent of them sent staff members to College Board meetings and 35 per cent of them used one or more Advanced Placement programs. It seems quite clear that high school grades and the recommendation of the principals, once major criteria in college admission, have given way in many if not most institutions to an examination of College Board scores. Even in the case of independent secondary schools, as reported in Chapter 8, performance on the College Boards is thought by headmasters to be the most important criterion for college admission.

5. National programs have established a new pattern for the in-service education of teachers. Not long ago, local school districts and near-by universities shared in the in-service task. The program was ordinarily not very systematic nor significant; teachers attended late afternoon or evening classes or workshops, and occasionally enrolled in a summer session; about to the extent that advancement on the salary schedule required. This has now been altered appreciably, especially in science, mathematics, foreign language, and guidance. In 1962 alone the NSF allocated 41 million dollars for institutes, most of which were for secondary school teachers. Additional institute funds have been provided under provisions of the NDEA. In both programs teachers are paid to attend the institutes.

Nor have these institutes lacked registrants. For all urban schools studied in Chapter 7, 69 per cent of the schools had had one or more teachers attend a mathematics institute, 79 per cent a science institute, 50 per cent a language institute, and 50 per cent a guidance institute. Thus, for many secondary school instructors, inservice education means paid attendance at a year-long or summer institute at which a new high school course, or in some cases alternate courses, of a national curriculum program are examined.

Clearly, local in-service programs of the future will have to reckon with the scope, prestige, and resources available to these national programs. Moreover, social studies and English teachers are wondering when comparable programs in their own areas are to get under way.

6. National programs have altered school plant planning and construction. Since 1958, NDEA has obligated about 600 million dollars for various programs of which about 300 million was for minor remodeling and equipment having to do with science, mathematics,

foreign language, and guidance.[2] For all urban schools reported in Chapter 7, 82 per cent had made use of NDEA provisions for science, 63 per cent for mathematics, 74 per cent for language, and 73 per cent for guidance.

Superintendents and school boards have become rather ingenious in building new school buildings so that they might use NDEA funds to "remodel" and equip the rooms. The nature of this remodeling and equipping, it seems reasonable to suspect, has been guided by national programs, found in course content revision programs or institutes for teachers or both.

7. There has been differential use of the national programs. Utilization of four national programs in 240 Illinois high schools has been shown in Chapter 7. The analyses include differences by socio-economic levels as determined by the occupations of the people in the school community, by the rural-urban character of the school community, and by enrollments in the high schools. Actually, enrollment and rural-urban classifications result in very similar groupings.

Schools in communities where professional and managerial people are numerous, and thus higher on the socio-economic scale, make significantly greater use of: (1) NSF programs in content revision and institutes, (2) NDEA programs in remodeling and teacher training fellowships and, (3) College Board programs, than do schools in lower socio-economic levels. Only with respect to utilization of National Merit programs do the differences with respect to socio-economic levels appear to be insignificant. In terms of the rural-urban categories, urban schools make greater use than do rural schools of NSF mathematics content revision and institutes, of NDEA remodeling and institute programs, and College Board programs. The same tendency exists for NSF content revision and institute programs in science, but the differences were not significant at the one per cent level. Again, the National Merit program was used by nearly all schools in all classifications.

Rural schools appeared to be low users of most of the programs. Suburban schools were the high users of NSF and College Board, and most NDEA programs. Only in mathematics and language remodeling did Chicago schools equal or exceed suburban schools. In a number of instances, utilization by Chicago schools was almost as low as the utilization by rural schools. It seems rather clear that high

---

[2] U. S. Office of Education, *Financial Assistance Programs* (Washington: Government Printing Office, 1962).

schools with a high proportion of college-bound students are the chief consumers of the benefits of the national programs.

8. National programs have given the public a new measuring stick with which to evaluate schools. As noted in Chapter 4, lay groups and school board members are prone to judge the effectiveness of a school by the number of semi-finalists, finalists, and scholars a school places in National Merit competition. This tendency persists in spite of the evidence that success in National Merit competition is rather highly correlated with the socio-economic status of the families from which the high school students come. The drive to produce winners has led many schools to inaugurate coaching programs designed to help students do well on the National Merit tests.

The College Boards, too, have provided an objective measure of high school achievement. Students who rank well on the College Boards have a good chance for admission to the prestige colleges. In an upper middle class community, few things are seen as more important than the ability of a high school to help many of its seniors place high on the College Boards. For most communities, these two measures of high schools have been available less than ten years. Such measures clearly influence school-community relations.

9. Apparently, many people do not recognize or will not acknowledge the impact of the national programs on the schools. Despite the evidence presented in Chapter 7 that four national programs were affecting in many ways the 240 high schools included in the study, about one-half of the people ascribed "some" influence to NSF and NDEA; the other half tended to split between "little or no effect" and "great" influence. With respect to NSF, almost one-third of the rural respondents gave no response to the question.

With respect to College Boards and NMS programs, respondents recognized even less influence. Almost two-thirds of the respondents characterized the influence of such programs as having "little or no effect." The evidence summarized above suggests that the national programs have had a greater impact than high school principals were disposed to admit.

Conclusions

It seems clear that for the first time in our history, education is made an explicit aspect of our national interest. NSF was given authority to "develop and encourage the pursuit of a national policy for the promotion of basic research and education in the sciences." The

NDEA had as its stated purpose "to provide substantial assistance in various forms to individuals, and to States and their subdivisions, in order to insure trained manpower of sufficient quality and quantity to meet the national defense needs of the United States." While there may be a certain amount of sacred rhetoric in these two statements, there is clear recognition on the part of the President, the Congress, and many other national leaders that education is necessary in the production of trained manpower, and that trained manpower is indispensable to an industrial nation.

National programs, public and private, do appear to be having a decided impact upon the secondary schools of the nation. To be sure, there is little legal prescription in all of this; no high school is required to provide a language laboratory. Even so, the pressure from neighboring school districts, state departments of education, aspiring parents, and ready money to assist in the purchase of the equipment make the pressure very hard to resist. Nor would we suggest that these influences are pernicious; the language laboratory may be exactly what was needed to improve language instruction. Our only point is that there are many influences, and they are pervasive.

Many of the national programs tend to reinforce each other. NSF, NDEA, CEEB, and NMS, for the most part, are aimed at strengthening the college preparatory function of the high school. While science, mathematics, foreign language, and educational guidance have received more emphasis than the remainder of the program, the work of the College Boards, particularly the Advanced Placement programs, go beyond these areas. It seems quite clear, however, that the programs make a much larger contribution to college preparation than they do to vocational training or general preparation for citizenship.

Since college preparation is the central theme of the national programs, they have much greater appeal to communities with a high proportion of college-bound students. This was clearly demonstrated in the differential use made of the programs when the communities were viewed in terms of socio-economic levels or in terms of rural-urban characteristics. For a fair proportion of our high school population, the increased academic rigor of our programs probably represents a real gain. For those who must go into the blue collar jobs however, no national programs are being as extensively utilized.

There does seem to be a growth toward the standardization of high school programs. The College Boards, now employed so widely, have, in a sense, become our national matriculation examination. Already the market is flooded with materials designed to help students cram for the Boards. Every university that gets an institute approved for teachers of science, mathematics, foreign language, or guidance must apply to an agency of the U. S. Government for support of the institute and must meet the criteria held by the officials of that agency. National study groups in physical science, mathematics, chemistry, and biology have prepared from one to three courses for each of the subjects. To be sure, teachers will make individual adaptations, but the standardizing influence of these courses seems rather clear.

There has been a shift in decision making from the local-state to the national level. For the most part, this is not a requirement growing out of new legal arrangements; legally, states still have plenary power in education and local school districts are still seen as the operating agencies of the states. But the fact remains that there are broad scale national curriculum programs which tend to supersede state and local efforts. There are institutes for teachers sponsored by national agencies which tend to dominate the field. There is one College Board examination which tends to be more persuasive than the recommendations of thousands of high school principals in terms of college admissions. To note this shift is not to disparage it. Perhaps localism in our schools has run rampant and the inability of most of our state departments to give forthright direction to education is well-known.

Many people refuse to recognize the nature or the extent of the influence emanating from the national programs. This phenomenon may have two explanations. First, school people and laymen alike have been strongly indoctrinated with localism. Bailey[3] found this to be one of the real depressants in securing state aid for education in the Northeast. We suspect it operates at the national level as well. Second, most school people have fancied themselves as educational "leaders." With such an orientation, they have some difficulty in recognizing that they need or actually take direction from agencies at a more distant level of government.

Some Implications

Our examination of national programs for education has caused us to speculate about possible implications, and we would like to share a little of that thinking. To begin with, we strongly suspect that these national influences will continue and perhaps exert even

---

[3] Stephen K. Bailey et al., *Schoolmen and Politics* (Syracuse: Syracuse University Press, 1962).

greater influence than they do now. Several circumstances seem to support this position. If, as we contend, education is now part of the national interest, or more specifically, if the character and quality of secondary school programs is related to our national well-being, the federal government will not ignore what is happening in the schools.

Other circumstances contributing to national participation in education include the mobility of our population, the differential financial ability of the states, and the reluctance of most state legislatures to finance special projects needed by urban school districts. Most state legislatures are still dominated by rural legislators and these people have difficulty comprehending the need of New York, Chicago, and other cities for a massive and expensive new program for pupils in deprived neighborhoods. Such programs, when they come, we suspect, will be financed more by the federal than by state governments.

In the national programs for education, we think we detect a transition in policy making for American education. Until recently, schoolmen individually and through their associations were rather influential with Congress and with the various federal agencies having to do with education. We suspect, however, that in the last decade or so, public schoolmen have become less influential and university scholars have become more influential.

The calling of the university scholar to the policy-making level may be what is behind the use of the National Science Foundation as a second U. S. Office of Education with lavish support from Congress. In terms of public support, it should be noted that NSF has appealed to the scientific community, not to the school community. The National Defense Education Act, on the other hand, was oriented to the school community. The contrast between these two programs has been treated by Marsh and Gortner.[4] They ascribe the differences between NSF and NDEA to private and public orientations respectively. We think the contrast between the scientific orientation of NSF and the school orientation of NDEA is more significant.

In further support of the emergence of university scholars as policy makers in secondary education, we suspect the PSSC has done more to change the teaching of physical science than all previous efforts at local and state levels. We suspect that a half dozen college presidents are influencing American secondary education more than

---

[4]Paul E. Marsh and Ross A. Gortner, *Federal Aid to Science Education: Two Programs* (Syracuse: Syracuse University Press, 1962).

a comparable number of leading superintendents of schools. We note that the last two commissioners of the U. S. Office of Education have been university people, not public schoolmen. We are not too surprised to learn that the scientific advisor to the President has been instrumental in convening educational conferences.

All of this argues for a new alliance between schoolmen and university scholars. With the explosion of knowledge, the subject matter specialists are indispensable to the proper planning and operation of school curricula. There is still a place for those who understand the psychology of learning and for those who know about organizations and their direction, but the content specialist can no longer remain out of the picture. This new alliance may be a rather uneasy one for a time, but we think both sides must help shape it.

We would make a final point. We believe a new partnership among local, state, and federal governments is in the making. Actually, we have never had the discrete separation of powers that some people ascribe to our system. Grodzins, as noted in Chapter 1, has pointed out that in a federal plan, functions are shared at each level of government. Perhaps what we are saying is that clearer recognition of this sharing should emerge and the limitations of localism and state rights will become more apparent to more people. In this new partnership, a means of assessing the educational needs of the nation and a way of programming that will utilize the best offices of all levels of government must emerge. The hard case in the development of this program will be a mutually acceptable method of approaching the problem of financing the schools.

We suspect that the federal government will continue to provide categorical aid for certain critical programs such as the improvement of slum schools, and for large-scale projects such as the training or retraining of teachers.[5] We think that national programs under government auspices might be coordinated more effectively. The U. S. Office of Education might be strengthened and given a greater role in such coordination. We are not disposed to suggest the elimination of private national programs such as NMS and CEEB, but we think that the effect of such programs, as well as the public programs, should be continually assessed. Finally, we see the urgent need to forge a new partnership of local, state, and federal agencies in place of yearning for the return of yesteryear.

---

[5] See: Francis S. Chase, "Some Effects of Current Curriculum Projects on Educational Policy and Practice." *School Review.* (Spring, 1962), 132-147.